STILL HEALING

Still Healing

A Doctor's Notes on the Magic
and Misery of a Life in Medicine

Rosalind Kaplan, MD

MINERVA RISING PRESS
Glen Ellyn

Copyright © 2025 Rosalind Kaplan

All rights reserved. No part of this book may be reproduced in any form or by any electronic or mechanical means, including information storage and retrieval systems, without permission in writing from the publisher, except by reviewers who may quote brief passages in a review.

ISBN: 978-1-950811-22-9

Cover Image by Kelly Sikkema
Design by Brooke Schultz

Printed and bound in USA
First Printing January 2025

Published by Minerva Rising Press
864 Western Avenue
Glen Ellyn, IL 60137
www.minervarising.com

Still Healing	1
War Stories	5
Bag of Bones and Box of Knees	9
Keep Your Pants On	18
Oxy	42
Brain Surgery	52
Dancing with Death	72
Dream Logic	83
Some Matters of Choice	106
To A Patient	124
Shedding My Coat	127
A Diary of Calamities	165
Detach	183
Grow Old Along with Me	197
More Magic, Less Misery	221
Luck of the Draw	227
Reprise of Shedding My Coat	230
Acknowledgements	249
Acknowledgements of Previous Publications	251

Author's Note

The events depicted in this memoir are all true and reported as I can best remember them. I acknowledge that my memory may be skewed or inaccurate; this is the nature of memory, but I have reconstructed events to the best of my ability.

Many of the names and identifying characteristics of people I have written about have been changed. All names of patients have been changed to protect privacy. The academic and medical institutions for which I worked have not been named. I was employed by more than one Philadelphia area hospital system in the time period written about, and recollections of employment-related events may be from any of these institutions or composites. Anything I have written is not intended to impugn or disparage any entity, group, or individual, but to instead illustrate the culture, trends, and conditions of the us healthcare system as a whole.

This collection began as separate essays about different aspects of medicine and my medical career. As a group, I hope that they not only shed light on my own medical career but also give a view of the changing landscape of medicine and healthcare in the us over the last few decades.

PROLOGUE

Still Healing

My relationship with practicing medicine is a rocky one, much like a troubled love affair. In many ways, it *has* been a love affair. I love the art and science of medicine, and I always have. There is nothing better than the part of medicine that I call "doctoring," the actual care of the patient. In doctoring, I am using my knowledge of science and technology, combined with my attention and presence (what many people refer to as bedside manner) to improve another person's health and maybe even their life.

I chose the road of becoming a general internist, a doctor who takes care of adult patients, whole adult patients, rather than specializing in one organ system, because I loved the idea of doctoring so much. While the goal of medical care is often to cure a patient, it's not always possible, but in doctoring, it is possible to heal even when we can't cure. In standing with a patient when they are suffering, in being there for them, healing is always possible.

Sadly, however, it turns out that being a doctor isn't often about doctoring, at least not in the modern version of medical practice in the United States. And that's where the troubles in my relationship with medicine lie. There's the part I love but also a big chunk I hate. That hateful piece is in the administration of healthcare, what we call "the system": the business, the finances, the politics, and much of the culture.

When I chose medicine as my career thirty-five years ago, I was enamored with the idea of life-long learning, a community of like-minded colleagues, and the ability to help others with the knowledge I garnered. All this, along with a secure financial future, made this career path appealing.

Of course, I expected sacrifice to get to my goal. I would have to work very hard. There would be long hours and a great deal of responsibility, both in training and in my long-term career. That was okay with me. I loved a challenge. I knew I could do the work. I was good with people and wanted to help others. I had this.

Well, maybe not. I don't think anyone really knows what they're getting into when they sign up for medical school and residency training. I probably accurately understood what the intellectual demands would be, but no matter what anyone told me, there was no way to comprehend the physical and emotional ones I'd be undertaking. The only way to find out was to do it.

During all the years of grueling and often merciless training, the long hours of study for board exams, the loss of sleep and leisure, during the decades of beating up on myself for not being good enough and smart enough, through all the hardest times, I banked on getting something back. Not just financial security, which could have been achieved in other, less soul-wrenching endeavors. I banked on professional satisfaction, a sense that I was doing something good with my life. I expected positive interactions with my patients, autonomy to make decisions, and some modicum of respect.

I found all that and more at many junctures in my career. But just as the world is always in flux, so is healthcare. The administrative aspects of medicine were always there, and I was aware of a slow erosion of autonomy from early in my career. Electronic record-keeping, which allowed patient records to be shared across health systems, accelerated that change. At some point, it seems there was a head-on collision between corporate culture and the doctor-patient relationship. You can probably guess which one suffered the most damage. A lot of the doctoring in medicine was lost along the way.

Still, like an addictive drug, medicine kept its hold on me. For one thing, my physician identity was deeply ingrained from years of training and practicing. But more than that, I couldn't give up the occasional high of a really good doctoring moment, the thrill when the art and science, the technology and personal presence came together.

But what happens when the practice of medicine becomes more misery than magic for doctors? How can doctors heal patients when they themselves are wounded by the system? What happens to those doctors, and what happens to patients? We were already at this breaking point years ago, when the rate of physician burnout exceeded fifty percent, and were beginning to see the fallout of physician shortage and patient dissatisfaction.

Add a global pandemic that created a crisis in both physical and mental health for the world. Stir. Then add the stress and casualties of climate crisis and blend well. Fold in social injustices that result in barriers to care and demoralization of both patients and doctors. Bring to a rolling boil, and there you have the U.S. healthcare system in its present iteration.

I don't have answers to the problems, but I know that healthcare needs healing. I can only tell my own story, and hope it adds to the collective voice calling for change.

ONE

War Stories

We tell war stories, we doctors do. Like veterans, we talk about our most harrowing times: the worst nights on call; the time we stayed awake, working, *keeping someone alive* for thirty-six or forty-two hours at a stretch; the time we almost died driving home because we couldn't stay awake any longer and nodded off at the wheel. We commemorate the most gruesome gunshot wound we saw as a student, the youngest patient we lost in a code blue as a resident.

Three or four decades may have gone by since the events we recount, still we will find an opportunity to bring up the time the attending threw a scissors at us in the O.R. (Operating Room), or the time blood started spurting out of our patient's esophagus, splattering the ceiling in the I.C.U. (Intensive Care Unit).

When we get together in groups, the tales are told on endless replay: Remember that patient with the maggots in her bedsores? The drug addict who shot heroin into his central line when he was on my watch?

We like to talk about our intimate relationship to the brokenness: the brokenness of our fellow humans, of the system, of equipment, of the world. I say I am proud of the night I took a ten-year-old bullet out of a man's leg in urgent care. It was eroding out through his skin, pus surrounding it, we were in the first weeks of the pandemic, and the E.R.s (Emergency Rooms) were packed with COVID patients. So, I did something I wouldn't ordinarily do without the equipment and the backup of the hospital.

Everyone talked about it; for a moment there, I was "badass," a cowboy, a renegade. It made me seem more interesting than I really am—an aging, nerdy doctor of internal medicine, a woman who would rather read a novel than go to a party and who can't handle more than one drink in an evening.

What is it about the brokenness that makes us want to return to it over and over when we are together? Well, what are war stories, after all, except the recounting of trauma? We act like our proximity to the brokenness makes us unbroken, whole, unbreakable. Like flexing those trauma muscles over and over makes them tougher and stronger. But isn't it really the opposite? The closer we sit to the brokenness, the more broken we are?

We think that, somehow, all these terrible debacles make us more resilient. Look at all I've experienced! I shocked someone with a defibrillator nine times in one evening! Look what I can handle! Look how immortal I am! But when I really let myself remember . . . when I go back to what it felt like then, I know it didn't bring resilience.

I am alone, the only doctor covering an interminable night of suffering at the cancer hospital affiliated with my medical training institution. A patient with lymphoma, now in kidney failure and heart failure after chemotherapy wreaked havoc on his body, has an arrhythmia.

I know next to nothing about chemotherapy, and less about the damage it has done to my patient's heart, but I am well-versed in the protocol for treatment of this abnormal heart rhythm. I begin instituting it, but I'm scared. I'm scared that I'm not going to get this right, that this man's chance at beating his cancer is going to end with my inexperience, my ineptitude, and that I am going to inflict suffering rather than alleviate it.

I'm sweating and cold at the same time as I inject medications into my patient's central intravenous line, and my hands shake as I apply the defibrillator pad to my patient's chest. He is sedated, not consciously aware of the jolt of electricity, but his body jerks, and I imagine it registering in some deep animal part of his brain. After all the medications are in, and I have increased the voltage of the shocks and his heart continues beating at an unsustainable rate, I page the cardiologist on call. He tells me I must place a pacemaker if the next round of shocks doesn't convert the rhythm. I don't know how. I have only seen this done once, but he tells me I will have to—it will take too long for him to get to the hospital so he can do the procedure. He talks me through it on the phone.

Once I get the pacer to capture, I should feel jubilant. I have *saved a life*. But I'm not. At first, I am shaking and cold and numb. Then I reach the on-call room, lock the door behind me, the nausea hits, and I vomit and quake for the next half hour while ignoring a page from a nurse about another patient with a fever. All I want is to go home and never return, never have another night on call, never be responsible for another life. I am not even ready to take responsibility for my own life.

This night will stay with me and become a war story. This night, and the night my patient bled to death in the radiology suite while I tried to force more blood into his dying body by squeezing the bag holding the packed red blood cells. These nights and the time a patient bit me in the E.R. That patient and the needle-stick injury that gave me hepatitis. All that and the woman who screamed, "Fuck you!" and spat at me a hundred times because I wouldn't refill her pain medicines, and the man who had a psychotic break in my waiting room and smeared feces on the walls until the cops came and took him to psych crisis.

Our traumas bind us doctors to each other, especially if we've been in medicine for a long time. "You know, the residents don't even have to stay overnight anymore. They have work hour limits, but when I was a resident, we didn't eat or sleep or go to the bathroom for whole days . . ." I hear this coming from my mouth, from the mouths of my colleagues, and I cringe.

It's not that we want these younger doctors to suffer as we did. We lobbied for change. We want things to be better. We just need to return, over and over, to our own suffering, and pretend, one more time, that we might be whole, unbreakable, badass, when really we are broken, broken down, tired, mourning. We lost the innocence that comes from steering clear of trauma until it comes to find you. Instead, we walked directly through trauma's door and let it lock us in. We need to return to the moments of trauma over and over, turn them around, see them with a different slant, as though the retelling might break the lock.

TWO

Bag of Bones and Box of Knees

July 1983, anatomy lab. We are grouped, alphabetically, in fours. My group is all last names starting with B-a, but we know each other by our first names—Jim, Mitch, Gavi, and me, Rosalind, but I go by Roz and pray nobody will call me Rozzie like my family still does.

Now, in July of our first year of med school, the four of us don't know each other well. By the end of the semester, we will. We will learn odd things about each other, like how we each hold a scalpel, whether we are meticulous or sloppy, our views on the afterlife. We won't necessarily be friends. We won't ask the ordinary questions of each other that people do on the way to friendship, like where we grew up and what we like to eat.

We don't talk about food in anatomy lab. Even thinking about food is impossible for me in this environment, where the air is infused with the rancid, oily smell of formaldehyde and we slice into human muscle, which doesn't look much different than chicken meat. I will stop eating chicken after the first day of dissection. I never liked liver much, but the idea of liver as food will also become unfathomable soon. Why would anyone eat an organ that filters toxins from the rest of the body? In fact, I will have little appetite at all my first semester of med school as I smell, and therefore taste, formaldehyde everywhere I go.

The first day of anatomy, we stand at our assigned metal table, two on each side. Our cadaver lies on the table, swathed in a black tarpaulin. The professor, Dr. H, a crusty old Scotsman, was reportedly a world-famous orthopedic surgeon in his youth. He delivers a lecture on appropriate comportment around a dead body.

"Remember, these cadavers were people who donated their bodies to science so you could learn. Show them respect. Keep them covered when you're not working on them. I don't want to hear any crude comments about the looks of them. Any extra skin or fat or other parts you remove from your cadavers go in here so we can dispose of them properly."

He indicates a large black bucket of formaldehyde, a slop bucket of sorts.

"No body parts leave this room. Last year two breasts were found somewhere they shouldn't have been. Suffice it to say, any pranks like that will get you thrown out of this institution. I'll say no more on that."

I look around. Most of my classmates are staring at their shoes. *Would anyone in this room be that callous?* I wonder, and then answer myself. *Yes, probably.*

Decades later, when I am a faculty member at a medical school and my students have been introduced to the bodies as "human gifts" instead of "cadavers," I will think about the power of words and wonder whether the name we give to a dead body changes anything. I'll wonder if some med students still have the kind of cruelty and crudeness in them those "pranksters" did, or if this younger generation is more enlightened than we were.

Dr. H adds some safety precautions: always wear your gloves, don't point your scalpels or scissors at yourselves or each other, and a few initial dissection instructions. Then he tells us to remove the tarps.

Once uncovered, our cadaver, a woman, looks very small. She was obviously quite elderly at the time of death. Gaunt, shriveled, and wizened, she is the proverbial "bag of bones." I feel disoriented, slightly stunned by how *not* human she appears. As much as I want to look away, my eyes are riveted to this body. The stinging, sickly formaldehyde odor is making me dizzy. I briefly feel like I can't breathe.

I wonder for a moment if all dead bodies look so shrunken but remind myself this can't be true. When I'm able to break out of my hyper-focus, I look around at the other cadavers in the room, roughly a dozen of them. Ours is by far the smallest and thinnest. Some are much larger. Yet they all look equally alien.

"Look!" says Jim, breaking the awkward silence at our table. "There's a tag."

Sure enough, there is a tag attached to our cadaver's wrist. No name. Just *"Female, age 91."* Yes, she'd been old.

"Let's call her Viola," says Jim. "She looks like my great-aunt Viola." Nobody objects, so she becomes Viola.

(I'm sure that now, all these years later, naming the "human gifts" is frowned upon, but it was our own way of humanizing our cadaver, and I still think of Viola with reverence.)

"Okay, everyone," yells Dr. H over the din generated by the unveiling of the bodies. "Get out your dissecting kits. We're going to begin."

My lab partners and I are not to become a cohesive group. Jim and I gravitate to each other and become friends. With his earnest expression and bright green eyes, Jim is unfailingly optimistic, upbeat, and kind. I am more cynical, a way to cover my anxiety and sensitivity, but it makes me seem quick and funny. We are a good combination, supportive and non-competitive. Our plan is for both of us to succeed in med school, and we recognize the drive and talent to do so in each other. We sit together in class, socialize with the same group of people, and study together often.

Mitch hides behind his mop of dark curls and facial scruff. He is hard-edged and sarcastic, a "gunner" intent on showing up the rest of us. He often goes to the anatomy lab alone at night to study Viola. He never invites a study partner.

Gavi is at the opposite end of the spectrum and seems oddly unconcerned with learning.

She often fails to appear for lab, and when she does show up, it is usually halfway through the dissection. We may, for instance, have cut into Viola's calf, exposed the gastrocnemius muscle, and started exploration of the saphenous vein. Perhaps we are looking for branches of the sciatic nerve, poring over our lab manuals and praying we haven't accidentally cut through the nerve tissue. Mitch is cocky, forging ahead without us. Jim is pointing at a strand of tissue, saying, "Is that it?" and I am replying, "I don't think so. I think that's vein, not nerve."

Suddenly, little redheaded Gavi appears in her street clothes. The rest of us are in our old jeans and tattered T-shirts that we have dedicated to the anatomy lab, and we leave these garments in our lockers after lab, to minimize the stench that chronically identifies us as first- year students. She points at an exposed body part and says, "Please tell me, what is that?" in her musical accent. We ignore her, having told her repeatedly that she needs to at least make an attempt at being a team player.

Dr. H has a harsh exterior, though I believe he may have a soft spot on the inside at least for the students who try hard. Rumor has it that he was much nicer before he lost his knees. Not his own knees. He still has those, though in his seventies, he walks with a limp which I would now refer to as an antalgic gait, a pattern indicating pain in the favored leg. But back then, his suffering hadn't occurred to me.

The story goes that, in his glory days, Dr. H was a pioneer in knee replacement. Even after he left orthopedics and became an anatomist, he lectured widely on the subject. He had a large collection of worn-out, arthritic kneecaps, cartilage, tendons, and ligaments that he'd removed from his patients. He brought these with him on his lecture circuit, in some sort of box, to demonstrate the horrible pathology present in his patients before he simply removed and replaced the injured parts.

Apparently, on one of his major overseas trips, the box, checked through with his luggage, disappeared, never to be seen again. It was one of the great losses of his life, one he never completely recovered from. A layer of crust settled over him then, and he barked more loudly and viciously at his students after that.

Early September, and our first "tag test" is administered. We are to enter the lab with a clipboard and pen. On the clipboard is a paper with blank lines, labeled one through twenty.

Throughout the room, cadavers have been tagged with corresponding numbers, and we must properly identify the tagged structures. They may be muscles, bones, nerves, organs, or blood vessels. We are only partway through the dissection, so only structures we have studied are included on the test.

I'm ready. I'm on. I move from table to table, easily recognizing each part. Sesamoid bone of the hand, saphenous vein, pyriformis muscle...Wait, what is this? I've never seen this before. It's internal, attached, it seems, to the genital organs in a male cadaver. My group has a female cadaver, but of course I studied the male pelvic anatomy in the book, so why can't I identify this? Nothing I studied looked anything like this, a thick, muscular structure, bisected in the sagittal plane. I have no idea, so I take a wild guess: the "crus" of the penis, a word I skimmed over in my reading, something that has to do with the point of attachment of the penis to the rest of the pelvis. Something I'm pretty sure is *not* an internal organ, so I'm almost certain it's wrong, but I don't have any other answer.

After the test, in the locker room, I ask Jim. "That was the bladder!" he exclaims.

"No!" I gasp. "Viola's bladder didn't look *anything* like that."

Viola's bladder was tiny, thin walled, with barely any muscle at all. It looked so completely different from that tagged structure that I would have sworn they were different organs, yet of course Jim is right, given the position and attachments. I fall to the floor, laughing hysterically at my own foolishness.

"Dr. H is gonna love this one," I choke, telling Jim what I wrote. He looks at me and bursts into laughter as well.

Two days later, I get my corrected test paper back—ninety-five percent, an A, but a note from Dr. H next to my error saying, "What the hell were you thinking, girl?" All these years later I cringe, partly at my stupidity, and partly at being called "girl" by my med school professor. At the time, I thought nothing of the moniker. Realizing this now, I wonder how I could have been so oblivious.

By the end of October, we are finished dissecting the limbs and midsection, and have moved on to the thorax. After many late nights studying, too much coffee, and a severe lack of sunlight, we are all feeling ragged. We've figured out that, no matter how hard we work, there is too much to learn, not just in anatomy, but in all our classes. We hope what we absorb will be enough and worry it won't.

Our anatomy quartet is not getting along well at all. Jim and Mitch are barely tolerating each other. Jim says Mitch is an asshole and a cutthroat. Mitch calls Jim "faggot" under his breath during lab one day.

Gavi has attempted to befriend me, inviting me to Shabbat dinner with her and her husband. They are Iranian Jews who fled Khomeini's violently anti-Semitic regime. As another Jewish woman, she looks to me for a sense of solidarity and understanding. But I am too self-absorbed at this point to notice her isolation and homesickness.

She complains to me that some of our classmates believe she was only admitted to the med school on account of her husband, who is a rising star in the surgery residency. She wants to make sure I know she got in on her own merits. I don't doubt this, but I find it hard to like her when she doesn't pull her weight in anatomy lab. Other students have told me that, in the same way, she lurks on the edges of her pathology lab and her study group. I could tell her this; it would benefit her to know, but I don't. I'm too nice, too nonconfrontational. Instead, I turn down the invitation, and shrug off her comments.

Meanwhile, I have made a big mistake with Mitch, and I'm paying for it. I drank too much at a post-exam party a couple of weeks earlier and let him kiss me in a stairwell. It meant nothing to me; I have a serious boyfriend in another city. I don't know what it meant to him, but I know the kiss felt aggressive and hostile. I fled the stairwell right afterward, so it ended there, but now he leers at me across the dissecting table. I feel the heat of his gaze. I ignore him, pretending to be deeply engrossed with my lab manual and scalpel. I've told no one, not even Jim, and I can only hope Mitch has been equally circumspect.

End of December, right before Christmas break. The dissection is essentially complete, except for the sinuses and cranium. The brains have been removed from the cadavers for separate examination in the neuroanatomy section of the course in the spring. Our job today is to split the skull to examine the inside of the head. I've read the required section in the manual. Splitting the skull requires first an axe and then a saw.

I change in the locker room and head up to lab feeling slightly panicked and a little queasy. I reach my table and find . . . nobody. I look at the clock, and it is time for lab to start. None of my three partners are there. All around the room, groups are preparing to begin, speaking in hushed tones, laughing nervously, picking up their axes. I have uncovered Viola, but I stand, paralyzed, at her head, alone.

I glance at the lab manual. I read the instructions over and over: "Split the skull with an axe along the sagittal plane."

Me? By myself? I hear splintering bone and then the scraping sound of sawing around me. Still, I stand unmoving.

The next thing I know, Dr. H is standing next to me. "What the hell's the matter with you?" he bellows.

"I . . . well, I'm not sure . . . my partners aren't here . . . I've never used an axe . . ." I stammer.

"Well, if you're not going to do it, I'll do it for you!" he yells.

He picks up the axe and in a clear, fell swoop, whacks Viola's head apart. I watch him lift the saw, but I can't stay. For the first time in anatomy lab, I can't take it. I run into the hallway, slamming the door behind me. I stand against the wall, breathing in the hallway air, air not completely saturated with formaldehyde. I slide down the cool cinder block wall, and sit on the tile floor, head in my hands.

At first, I think Dr. H must be without a soul to do what he just did. Then I wonder. I wonder what it must be like to have cut open hundreds, maybe thousands, of bodies, both dead and alive, to have removed and replaced parts, to have kept all those human bones in a box and treasured them and then lost them. I wonder what it must be like to lose one thing after another as you try to pass on a lifetime of skill and knowledge to others, including frightened first-year medical students. I think about the fact that Dr. H cut the skull for me instead of forcing me to do it myself.

I know I must get up and go back into the lab soon. I must learn to do what must be done. But while I still have the luxury of this moment, I breathe.

THREE

Keep Your Pants On

We got engaged in the supply closet of the medical I.C.U. as ventilators huffed and hummed beyond the closet door and a bleeding patient received multiple transfusions on the other side of the wall. This was how our "real life" began—the beginning of a marriage, the launching of our careers, the building of our life and family together.

At the time we decided to marry, Larry and I were both in the thick of our Internal Medicine residency programs. We were sleep-deprived, overworked, and underpaid, conditions which seem incompatible with such a decision. Yet life moves inexorably forward, no matter what one's circumstances. We were in our late twenties; I suppose we were biologically programmed to mate, nest, and reproduce. Sociologically, we were primed to marry, settle down, and have a family. That our career paths weren't conducive to these goals became immaterial. All of it—finishing our medical training, passing our board certification exams, finding jobs, getting married, having babies—all of it was equally pressing and crucial and *necessary*, at that juncture in time.

I first met Larry in his living room during my third year of medical school at the University of Pennsylvania, and his fourth year at Temple University School of Medicine. It was a chance meeting. I was there with my classmate, Beth, who was dating one of Larry's housemates, and when we arrived, Larry was not there. But as soon as he appeared that night, I knew he was different from the other men I'd dated.

I'd arrived in Philadelphia to start medical school in 1983. I was still involved with my college boyfriend then, but that didn't last long. He started law school in New York, and our worlds quickly diverged.

The medical environment, especially thirty years ago, when medical school classes were still predominantly male, was teeming with men. I dated a few of them in the next couple of years. Mike, an anesthesia resident, was laser-focused on his work, but alarmingly indecisive in other areas. He would shop for clothes, then return everything he bought. I started to wonder when he would decide to return me. Dan, a pediatrics intern, was so chronically sleep-deprived he couldn't stay awake through a movie or a meal. I decided he'd benefit more from a nap than my companionship. Wes, a neurology resident, called me "Gorgeous" instead of using my name. Unfortunately, he had a fiancée in another city but neglected to tell me until she showed up unexpectedly one day, which made me wonder if he didn't even *know* my name.

Maybe the reason I wasn't meeting anyone truly available was that I wasn't truly available. In the first couple of years of med school, I was mostly thinking about, well, med school. I went to classes, study groups, and spent weekday evenings in the library. I volunteered at the community free clinic. I spent the little free time I had swimming at the university pool or socializing with my classmates. Men were a nice distraction, but I didn't think about romantic relationships as long-term commitments until I met Larry.

The night we met was a Saturday in February of 1986. Beth and I were looking for entertainment. It was snowing, so it seemed a good night to watch a movie, something we could do because her boyfriend, Zach, was one of the few people we knew who owned a VCR. When we arrived at his place, he was the only one home in the huge, drafty apartment that was part of an old fieldstone house typical of his Philadelphia neighborhood. A radiology resident at one of our med school's affiliate hospitals, Zach shared the apartment with four other guys—an assortment of medical students and residents from different area programs. He was happy to make use of his VCR, and we decided to rent a French drama called *Entre Nous*.

We had barely started watching when Larry appeared. The sound on the VCR was interrupted by loud clomping noises as he approached the apartment door and started kicking snow off his cross-country skis on the front porch. When Larry entered the apartment, Zach stopped the movie to introduce us.

Larry told us he'd been working a shift at the local food co-op and had taken advantage of the newly fallen snow to travel back and forth on his skis. He took off his parka and shook the snowflakes out of his curly dark hair. His jeans were encrusted with ice almost to the knees.

When I looked at his face, the first thing I noticed were red-rimmed glasses, which I thought unique. Even with his glasses on, though, the color of his eyes stood out. They were the darkest blue I'd ever seen, almost navy—the color of the ocean at dusk. I was drawn to his smile, too. He smiled with his eyes.

"I'll be right back," he said. "I just need to put on dry clothes."

We restarted the movie. When Larry returned in dry jeans, a sweater, and a pair of Birkenstocks over wool socks. He sat down next to me on the sofa. It wasn't awkward. In fact, it was comfortable, familiar. Who was this crunchy-granola, Birkenstocked man who worked at a food co-op? Definitely not my type. I was into edgier, more intense men. But I still thought Larry was cute, and for some reason, I felt like I already knew him. Or he already knew me...

I missed most of the end of the movie because Larry kept whispering questions to me.

Zach had told him I went to school with Beth. But in what year of med school was I? What rotation was I doing? Did I know what I wanted to specialize in? At what hospital had I done my Internal Medicine rotation? Where did I live?

As the evening got later, the apartment got colder.

"Yeah," Larry told me when I commented on the temperature, we can't really afford to heat this place, so we keep the thermostat at sixty-two degrees all winter."

The next thing I knew, I'd stuck my feet under Larry's legs for warmth. I didn't think about it. I harbored no intentions in this, at least no conscious intentions. I just felt comfortable with him; it seemed like a natural thing to do. He didn't appear surprised, so we sat there and talked with my feet under his butt until it was time for me to leave.

Later, a conversation would reveal that, for several years, our families lived in the same town in Central New Jersey. I was a baby then, and he a toddler. Our parents belonged to the same synagogue and ran in the same social circle. We'd likely been plopped into a playpen together at social gatherings. I attributed our instant adult comfort with each other to some kind of preverbal recognition.

Our first date was on Chinese New Year, so we headed to Chinatown. We talked easily, and I was attracted to him, but he didn't touch me—no handholding, no good-night kiss. Was he anxious? It didn't seem like it. Maybe, I reflected, he just wasn't into me.

He invited me out again, though, this time to a restaurant known for being "romantic." I wore a soft, cream-colored angora pullover, hoping it would make him want to touch me. I needn't have worried, as on the way out of my apartment building, on the landing of the stairs, he stopped and read me some lines of a poem, then kissed me. It was corny, but so sweet I couldn't help being impressed. Later, when I asked him why he'd been so hands-off on our first date, he said it was to show me respect.

By our third date, I believed we would someday be married.

How do you explain why you love someone? Back then, if you'd asked me, I don't think I could have explained.

Now, I can list the reasons I fell for Larry, but they don't do justice to the whole of what "love" means.

I felt safe. I could tell Larry anything. He made me laugh. He was nice to old people. He read books. He made great coffee. He went to the trouble to grind the coffee beans, and he sometimes added part of a stick of cinnamon into the grinder. When he bought me lingerie, it was made of soft cotton, instead of the sticky, shiny polyester most guys favored, because he believed that comfort mattered as much as beauty. He loved dogs. He drove a manual transmission. He knew an astounding amount about music, even the most obscure bands like Wall of Voodoo and The Plimsouls. He knew the right words to all the songs that everyone else wasn't sure about.

Larry: "You know that Creedence Clearwater Revival song, 'Bad Moon on the Rise'?

Everyone thinks the words are 'There's a bathroom on the right.'"

Me: "Wait, you mean I've been singing the wrong words all these years?"

Of course, we talked about medicine. We shared our calling, our passion, but it didn't dominate the relationship. It was just another part of the whole picture.

The Match is a computer program by which almost every fourth-year medical student's fate is determined. Once students decide what specialty they want to pursue, they apply to residency programs that interest them. If a program is interested in an applicant, an interview is the next step.

After interview season, for which some students travel all over the country, "rank lists'" are compiled. The programs rank the applicants they interviewed, and the applicants rank the programs that interviewed them. The rankings are entered into the computer, *et voila!* On Match Day, sometime in the spring of the fourth year of medical school, each student receives an envelope with a binding decision inside.

Larry had submitted his rank list for the Match before he met me. His first choice for his Internal Medicine residency was the University of Michigan. By the time Match Day came, we'd only known each other a few months. I didn't think we'd make it as a couple if he matched in Michigan; I had another year of medical school to finish in Philly, and residency is hard enough without trying to manage a long-distance romance.

Fate intervened once again. He matched at his second choice, the Medical College of Pennsylvania in Philadelphia. I told him I was sorry his first choice had not come through, but I really wasn't sorry at all. If he was disappointed that Michigan had not chosen him, he didn't let on. The computer had made the decision that we would stay together, at least for the foreseeable future.

Here's the thing about medical residency: no matter how ready you believe you are, nobody can prepare you for what will happen in those years of postgraduate training. Illness and injury and death and cure and recovery are wildly unpredictable events. There is no way to know how it will feel to be caught up in the grueling schedule of 24/7 patient care, punctuated with high drama throughout each day. There is no way to predict your reaction or how that reaction will affect the people around you. In our case, the combination of Larry's stress and my response to it was poison to our relationship.

Larry started his internship, the first year of residency, strong and confident, but doubt quicky crept in.

He spent the first few months of internship at the Philadelphia V.A. hospital, a grim and depressing institution, full to the gills with veterans from World War II, the Korean War, Vietnam, and whatever other battles they'd fought, now hospitalized with cancers and heart disease and dementia.

In 1986, smoking was still allowed in the V.A. hospital, and cigarettes were even sold in the gift shop. It was not uncommon to see groups of patients in the lobby, chain-smoking in their wheelchairs. Even the patients with lung disease would congregate over cigarettes, their oxygen turned off to prevent combustion. The head-and-neck-cancer survivors, despite the fact that their anatomy was already destroyed by tar and nicotine, smoked through their tracheostomies.

Just a glance at the VA lobby was enough to make the average person feel both sadness and revulsion—and that was just scratching the surface of the place. Possession of a medical degree didn't render one exempt from these feelings.

The V.A. was notoriously understaffed. The resident doctors were often left to do the work nurses or other ancillary staff should have been assigned. The amount of SCUT alone was crushing. (SCUT was originally an acronym for Some Clinically Useful Tasks—referring to blood draws, lab result retrieval, and replacement of intravenous lines and clogged feeding tubes—but long before my time, interns and residents riffed on the phrase, changing it to Some Common Useless Tasks, and the new acronym stuck.)

The inefficiencies and limitations of the system made the job of caring for patients there even more demoralizing. We used to quip that "STAT" at the V. A. meant "Some Time After Tuesday," but there was a sad truth to the joke. Obtaining a single x-ray or sub-specialty consult could be a Herculean task.

One day, after weeks of every-other-night call in the V.A. ICU, Larry accidentally drove down Market Street, one of Philly's major thoroughfares, in the wrong direction. Fortunately, the police stopped him before he caused an accident, and took pity on him when he explained his circumstances.

The V.A. military police, who provided security for the hospital, were not as kind. When, after a difficult night on call, Larry went to the cafeteria for coffee and found no creamer. He opened a single-serving milk carton, poured some milk in his coffee, and left the carton for the next sleep-deprived healthcare worker. A V.A. M.P. approached him at the cashier, handcuffed him, and put him in the brig (yes, the V.A. also had its very own jail cell!) for stealing milk. He stayed there for two hours until a supervising doctor noticed his absence on rounds and demanded his release.

Between the grueling schedule and these arbitrary extra punishments, Larry became irritable and angry. With little time for exercise or other hobbies, he had no good outlet for his emotions. At one point, he told me he'd expressed his hostility by throwing charts out the seventh floor on-call room window into a small, wooded area behind the hospital.

He had very little time to spend with me during those first months of internship. When we were together, he was often distracted or just cranky, and sometimes he fell asleep in the middle of dinner or even a conversation. We rarely went out. Looking back, it was all exactly what one would expect with the sort of work hours, sleep deprivation, and intense pressure he was experiencing. The only way a loving partner can help during residency is by being there, offering a meal or a soothing word, and quietly waiting out the storm. I was not that loving partner.

Instead of waiting out the storm, I walked away. Or to be more precise, I let myself be spirited away by a more available man, because I felt neglected.

I met Dave, a psychologist, in Philadelphia's Thirtieth Street Station while waiting to buy a train ticket. I was in the midst of an Internal Medicine sub-internship, a rotation during which I acted as an intern, but with more supervision, at the Hospital of the University of Pennsylvania. I was scheduled for overnight call in the hospital the night before Larry's sister's wedding. After a busy night with little sleep, I bolted out of the hospital and literally ran to the train station, still in my surgical scrubs and sneakers, to make the train to New Jersey.

Dave was standing in front of me in the line for tickets. He was a good-looking man, with bright blue eyes and shaggy dark blond hair. He wore jeans, a black leather jacket, and a camera slung around his neck. He was older than me, but I wasn't sure by how much. I could tell he was confident in himself by the way he stood—solidly rooted to the ground, as though he knew he belonged there. At twenty-five, and still a student, I never really felt like I belonged anywhere. Later, he would tell me he was thirty-six.

I think he was intrigued by my doctor garb, and he started a conversation. He had a sexy British accent. He flirted with abandon. I told him I wasn't available. He didn't really care. He behaved as though I fascinated him, and after an hour on the train with him, I didn't care either.

He asked for my number. I gave it to him, all the while knowing it was the wrong thing to do. After an evening with him in Philly, I decided he was my fantasy man, ready to save me from the drudgery of the complicated, sometimes unsatisfying relationship I was already in, and maybe from the complex life I'd chosen.

I didn't cheat on Larry. I told him I'd met someone. By then, he was so downtrodden that he hardly reacted, but I knew it was a hard blow, one that he experienced as another undeserved punishment. I'd just turned his mostly lousy intern year into a fully miserable intern year.

Dave was a crappy boyfriend. He played with my head—a trick that, as a psychologist, he was good at but never should have employed. After the first shiny days of new lust, he realized I wasn't what he really wanted. No matter; I was good raw material, so he tried to change me into what he preferred. His ploy was transparent, but my vision was distorted, so I didn't see through it at first.

He'd buy me an article of clothing, something beautiful—silken, pink, something that would look great on someone who wasn't me. I was strictly a denim and black leather boots type. He'd suggest I wear more makeup, dress more like an adult. He seemed to forget that I was a student, as much girl as woman at that point.

He took me to parties and introduced me to his friends, all more than ten years my senior, none of whom I had anything in common with. I felt like a zoo animal on display, as they tried to figure out what he was doing with me. Afterward, he critiqued my social skills.

While Dave tried to mold me into the girlfriend he desired, all I could think about was Larry. How he had loved me exactly the way I was. How easy it had been to be with him. How we understood each other without having to explain things. All I wanted to do was sit in the cane rocking chair in the corner of his bedroom while he sat on the bed, reading or strumming his guitar. With Dave, what I wanted to do was run away, but I'd let myself be convinced that if I would act right and look right, I could make this work. Anyway, it was too late for me and Larry.

One day I started an argument with Dave. I couldn't stand being judged and adjusted and reassessed by him for one more moment. The disagreement, which was over nothing, quickly turned ugly and accusatory, and then we were done.

At first, I thought I was bereft. After a few days, though, I noticed that I felt better than I had in a long time. Everything had gone to hell while I was with Dave. My work had suffered; I finished my pediatrics rotation with just a "Pass," while I'd achieved "Honors" or at least "High Pass" in my other rotations. My apartment was a mess, as I'd barely been there for months, just stopping in to get clean clothes or take a post-call nap. I hadn't been swimming, and I'd neglected my friendships. Now I was free to get my life back on track.

Later, a therapist would comment that my relationship with David had been like a strapless, bejeweled evening gown—something that was gorgeous for one evening, but uncomfortable and inappropriate and wholly unsustainable for the rest of life, while Larry and I were like your most worn-in, favorite pair of jeans—imperfect, a little rough around the edges, but what you choose to live in every day. She couldn't have been more accurate.

Once I put myself back together, I missed those worn-in jeans. I deeply regretted discarding them and longed to have them back. I found myself thinking about Larry all the time. I wanted to contact him but was afraid he wouldn't want to hear from me. When I tried calling, his phone just rang and rang. I didn't dare page him at the hospital. There was no email or texting back then, so I decided the only way to talk to him was in person.

It would have to be in the evening. He likely was on call every third night, and I didn't know his call schedule. He might well be at the hospital when I showed up. Or worse, what if he had a new girlfriend, and I arrived when he was with her? What if he told me to go away? Well, that was a chance I was going to have to take.

Feeling like a stalker, I drove to his apartment. His building was owned by a Vietnam veteran with PTSD. There was no intercom because disembodied voices frightened him. If Larry was home, he would have to come downstairs and open the door to the building to see who was there.

I waited until 8:30 p.m. Unless he was on call, he'd certainly be home by then. I rang the bell for his apartment, then rang again. When nobody came, I rang a few more times. Finally, I heard footsteps on the stairs, and moments later, he opened the door. He was standing there, hair tousled, his eyes glazed, in the ugly rust-colored terry cloth bathrobe his mother had given him for his birthday, the one we'd laughed at because of the hideous color, but he then wore anyway, because it was comfortable. His mouth dropped open when he saw me.

"What are you doing here?" He sounded tired and puzzled, but he didn't seem angry.

"I need to talk to you. I couldn't get you on the phone. I'm sorry for just showing up."

"I was on call last night. I was sleeping, and I'm really exhausted."

"I'm sorry. Can we talk for just five minutes?"

He hesitated, then stepped back to let me in. "Sure, but I really need to go back to sleep soon."

I followed him up to his apartment. I hated that apartment. Brown carpeting. His grandma Rose's blue flowered sofa. Larry's disinterest in aesthetics had frustrated me, but now it seemed just another charming quirk. I still wanted to change it, but not because I felt like Larry needed to change. Instead, I had the thought that a nicer environment would lift his spirits—something he wouldn't have thought of, but that I could have done for him.

"Do you mind if we sit in the bedroom? I need to lie down. I'm pretty dead," Larry said.

"No, that's fine." Secretly, I was happy. If he hated me, would he let me in his bedroom?

Besides, I could sit in the rocking chair.

It was surprisingly comfortable to be there, even five months after breaking up. To me, it still felt like home—he still felt like home—even in this awkward situation. I sat in the rocking chair, drawing my legs up under me. He lay on the bed, propped up on multiple pillows.

"So . . .?" he said. I detected combativeness in his tone, but I wasn't going to let it deter me.

"I made a terrible mistake," I started.

"Okay... Go on..."

"It was stupid. It wasn't fair to you. I felt abandoned because you were too busy to see me, and you were never around. And then this man comes along . . . and well, he turned out to be an asshole, if that's any comfort, and I missed you the whole time..."

"And now you're just showing back up, and you want me to pretend nothing happened?"

"No, I know you can't do that. But I'm asking if you'd think about forgiving me and trying again. Dave and I only lasted a couple months. I've been alone the last three months. Like I said, it was a terrible mistake. I know you were doing the best you could."

"I don't know. How am I supposed to trust you?"

"I'm not sure. I guess it will take time."

"This has been the worst few months of my life. I feel like shit. Part of that was you leaving."

"I know. I'm sorry."

"I'm too tired to think much more."

"Will you consider it?"

"Yes, I still love you."

"I still love you too."

We sat quietly for a few minutes. I rocked in the chair. Then I realized Larry was asleep.

We spent the last few months of Larry's internship year, and my last year of medical school, together, trying to re-establish trust. I was more understanding of his schedule and his fatigue.

He tried harder to be present when we had time together.

He was better adjusted to the demands of his program and managed to keep his cynicism at a dull roar. He only had one more trip to the brig, this time for trying to bring a bottle of champagne into the V.A. to celebrate the end of the last day of internship. When he finished the year, he got the "Crispy Critter" award for most burnt-out intern. I knew I'd contributed to his burnout, and I wasn't proud of it. But I also saw he was becoming a great doctor. I hoped I would be able to do that, too.

When I crawled back to Larry, I knew I needed to be more of an adult to be able to tolerate the frustrations and disappointments adult life, especially the particular adult life we'd chosen, might bring. In fact, the structure of medical training had been a perfect foil for avoidance of relationship and intimacy. We were all incredibly busy and focused on our goals to become good doctors, to fulfill the necessary requirements for graduation, and to get the residencies we wanted. We had little free time. Competition had been fostered in us since high school; cooperation was valued only secondarily. Our seemingly noble professional mission was often taken as an acceptable excuse for failed connections and botched communications in the interpersonal realm.

Now I was about to start residency, during which I would need to be tough and self- reliant, but also cooperative, and at the same time, I was determined not to mess our relationship up again. So much, I felt, was on the line.

Larry was a better partner to me when I was an intern than I had been to him. I was a wreck in my own way; I was just quieter about it than he had been. I did my thirty-six-hour shifts. At Temple, an inner-city hospital in the most impoverished zip code in Philadelphia, we treated ravages of not just disease, but of poverty, drugs, violence, and abuse. There were never enough resources or enough hours in the day to finish the work. Still, we tried.

I was exhausted and overwhelmed, just like Larry had been, but I could come home and tell him about it, and he understood. I would crash into a dreamless, motionless sleep after being on call, and he would wake me to feed me, then let me go back to bed. He never complained that I was inaccessible.

He initiated a discussion of moving in together. He had a little more time as a second-year resident, and he wanted to keep the relationship moving along. We were spending all our free time together, and I had to agree it was silly to keep two apartments only blocks away from each other.

I was unwilling to move into his ugly, brown-carpeted, intercom-less apartment, and my apartment didn't have the space to accommodate two of us and all our belongings. Finding an abode that we both liked, one proximate to the hospitals for both our residency programs, was a challenge. But one Saturday in early September, after rejecting scads of too-dark, too-small apartments, we found one that seemed to be in a good location. It was light, bright, and airy, and we would have signed the lease right then, but it was after five o'clock, and the Realtor's office was closed.

"I can have you sign it first thing tomorrow morning," she told us.

"I'm on call in the ICU tomorrow morning. I have to be there at seven," I replied, discouraged.

"I can sign it in the morning," said Larry. "No problem, we can add your name later."

The next morning, I arrived to chaos in Temple's Intensive Care Unit. The intern who had covered overnight signed out several unstable patients on ventilators, each needing very close attention.

"Also," he said, "Mr. A. is still here, stable now but may need a balloon pump later." Great. Mr. A. had end-stage congestive heart failure and was awaiting a heart transplant.

His heart was so damaged that, at any moment, it was possible he would need to have a device implanted to assist his left ventricle in pumping blood. While I knew that a cardiology fellow would come in to insert the pump if it became necessary, the idea that I might suddenly be responsible for keeping Mr. A. alive as his heart fibrillated and his blood pressure plummeted, waiting for the fellow get there, was daunting.

"And finally," continued my colleague, "I just admitted Mr. B., who is in the room right behind you, with a massive gastrointestinal bleed from a fistula between his aorta and his bowel. Surgery has seen him, but they aren't willing to take him to the O.R. until we get him medically optimized."

"I guess he's my first priority," I replied.

I spent the next several hours working on Mr. B. Without surgery, he would bleed to death, but he might also die on the operating table. I needed to improve his condition enough that the surgeons would have a chance to save him. I stood on a ladder holding two units of blood as high as I could, forcing them to run as fast as possible through the enormous IV catheters running into both of Mr. B's arms.

Once the transfusion was complete, I moved between rooms, adjusting ventilators and assessing Mr. A., the heart transplant patient, who did not appear to need a balloon pump at that moment.

Then back to Mr. B., to check his vital signs. Just then, my pager went off, indicating that I had a call on an outside line. I went to the nurses' station to pick it up. Larry.

"Hi, I can't really talk. I've got a unit full of unstable patients," I told him.

"Okay, I just wanted to tell you that I'm not going to sign the lease. I think the apartment is too far from the hospital for me. It's going to stress me out. We can look some more later in the week."

"Seriously? We've looked at every apartment this side of the city! I can't spend more time looking at apartments, and nothing suits you, anyway."

He'd picked the wrong moment to mess with me. I was a woman on a mission, getting things done, and he'd just undone something I thought was a fait accompli.

"Maybe you just aren't committed to moving in with me. Let's just forget it and stay in our apartments," I went on, irritable. I knew it was a threat, and that I wasn't playing fair. "I have to go."

"Wait!" he exclaimed, trying to keep me from hanging up the phone.

"I told you, it's chaos here. I have a patient exsanguinating. I'm going to go." I hung up. I did another quick run past the vents, titrating respiratory rates, and rounded on Mr. A. again. He didn't look any different. Back to Mr. B. Blood was coming out of his rectum faster than we could transfuse it into his arms. I ordered more blood from the blood bank.

I went out to the desk to chart what we'd done so far. Just then, I saw Larry walk in, carrying a pint of Ben and Jerry's Super Fudge Chunk ice cream. I glared at him from behind the desk.

"Can we talk? Just for a minute?" he asked.

"Not really! I have a lot going on here," I replied, pushing my mass of dark ringlets back from my face. I'd only been at work for a few hours and already my hair was in disarray, my cotton scrubs were rumpled, and my formerly white Reebok sneakers were spotted with blood.

"Please just give me a minute."

"You know I can't leave the unit."

"Then we can talk somewhere in here."

I looked around. "Everyone is going to hear every word," I told him.

"No, c'mon. We'll find some privacy."

He pulled me along toward the back of the unit and opened a door. The smell of pine cleaner and iodine blasted out of the cleaning supply closet. He grabbed my hand and pulled me inside, flipping on the light switch.

"Look, you better talk fast," I told him. "One patient is bleeding out, and another might need a balloon pump." I thought for a split second about how absurd my situation was. I was standing in a closet with my boyfriend while people were dying just outside the door. Did they keep balloon pumps in this cleaning supply closet?

"Okay, remember how you said on the phone that I'm not committed?" Larry asked.

"Yeah, well, you decided..."

"Wait, just let me finish. I want to show you I'm committed. Ask me to marry you."

"What?"

"I said, ask me to marry you."

"Larry, this isn't funny. I have to go. Mr. B. is exsanguinating." I gestured at my bloody shoes as proof.

"I'm not trying to be funny. Just ask me. Then I'll give you this ice cream, and you can get back to work."

"Oh, my God. This is ridiculous."

"Just ask me."

"Here? In a closet, while my patient is bleeding to death? Are you crazy?"

"Come on, just ask me, and then you can go take care of him."

"Fine. Will you marry me?" I said it flatly, deadpan. I thought he was playing some kind of joke on me. We had talked about living together but had never discussed marriage.

"Yes," he answered. "Here's the ice cream. Make sure you put it in the freezer. I'll see you tomorrow." He kissed me quickly, exited the closet, and walked away.

I didn't have time to think about our conversation. I was aware of feeling a little angry, thinking, *What kind of person jokes about marriage when you're already upset and you're dealing with exsanguination and failing hearts?* But maybe he was serious. In which case, he had just forced *me* to propose to *him* in a hospital closet then given me ice cream instead of an engagement ring. Although I had to give him some credit for choosing Super Fudge Chunk.

I put the ice cream in the break room freezer on the way to Mr. B. When I got to his room, the blood was just arriving, and so was the surgical resident.

The evening passed with a series of minor disasters, another admission or two, and the sad news that Mr. B. had not survived his surgery. I continued to adjust ventilators, IV drips, and medications through the night.

At the end of morning rounds, the ICU team tromped downstairs to the radiology reading room to look at our patients' studies. While there, I received another page to an outside line. This time it wasn't Larry. It was his father.

"Congratulations!" he greeted me.

I hesitated. I was confused, but so tired I wasn't sure what I was confused about.

"Welcome to the family!" he continued. "Have you picked a date yet?"

Larry's like that. He has his own way of doing things.

I suppose some women would feel cheated out of the proper, rehearsed proposal in the perfect romantic setting if this were their story. Getting engaged in the ICU supply closet was strange and a little macabre, and most definitely not idyllic. It wasn't even hot and steamy like a scene out of *Grey's Anatomy* (honestly, who has time for that while doing patient care?).

The truth is, though, that I love our story. It's kind of crazy, but it was us at that point in time—funny and sad and frenetic and with all the parts of ourselves, good and bad, mixed up together into a beautiful, complicated mess. I've told the story many times, at dinners and story slams, to new friends and eager medical students, and it invariably elicits laughter and a sort of reverence for the quirkiness of it all.

It's a great story. And I wasn't looking for the perfect, fairy-tale proposal. But look again, and you'll see a different kind of fairy tale, one that is darker and more twisted. In those moments in the supply closet, among the syringes and needles, we confronted so many conflicting and contrasting elements: elation and frustration, youth and death, love and loss, fantasy and fear, all inextricably bound together. That's a lot for any human being to process. So many emotions that it's hard to know what you feel. Or maybe it's so much that, after a while, you really can't feel anything at all.

Perhaps you're worried now that a marriage started in that way couldn't last, that with so many competing demands and distractions, we couldn't have possibly been attuned enough to each other to make it work. I, too, was worried about that in the early days of our marriage, but in fact, the circumstances seem to have cemented us together quite firmly. Medical training is, by its very nature, traumatic, and shared trauma is what made us part of the same culture, the same tribe, for better or for worse. I think we understand each other in a way that anyone outside of that culture can't. That we found joy and solace in each other amidst the chaos was a sort of grace, almost a miracle.

We had a difficult start. The many competing demands in our lives initially nearly burned us to the ground, but we managed to resurrect the relationship as a phoenix rising from the ashes. Or recycled like the good pair of blue jeans it was.

Blue jeans, when you think about it, are much more than just a pair of pants. They can be dressed up with a silk blouse and heels or worn with a T-shirt and work boots for the dirtiest jobs. Sturdy, washable, and mendable, they can take a lot of abuse and still have a long life. If you treat them with just a little bit of care, they get better over time.

Our relationship has lasted and mellowed and, I think, improved with time. Over the years, it has fit better at some times than at others. We have torn it and mended it again and again. We've frayed the edges, and the color has changed with wear, but we are still together thirty-five years later. We still find laughter and joy together during the good times, and we've learned how to offer a meal or a soothing word instead of running away during the bad. Sometimes we just have to be patient, to proverbially "keep our pants on." If we can do that, the hard times always pass.

FOUR

Oxy

In medical training, as a resident doctor, I spend a day each week in outpatient clinic with my own group of patients inherited from a resident who came before me and now has graduated to real life.

My patients have lousy insurance—Medicaid, or one of the cheap Medicare products; they are patients who can't afford commercial insurance. Those who can are placed in the clinics of attending doctors with more experience. My patients are sick with diabetes, heart problems, chronic lung disease, and back injuries—the products of stress, hardscrabble lives, bad luck, and food deserts.

They get good care from me, because I care. I am still fresh and new. I have energy and drive. I spend time with them; I dot my i's and cross my t's. I have a good preceptor in clinic to supervise my work, and I want to do it right.

I love clinic; it's a break from the horrors of the hospital. My patients will see me and then go home. They will come back and see me again in a month or a year, and some of them will do well, get better. But Helen N. isn't one of those who gets better. Helen is always the same.

I meet her my first week in clinic, a woman I remember as old, but when I think about it, she was younger than I am now. Maybe she was fifty, but a bad fifty, a battered, beaten-down fifty. Still, she comes to clinic in colorful clothes, her dark hair coiffed. Mostly, it's her eyes that are old. She is pleasant, well-spoken. She takes many pills—for blood pressure and sugar, anemia and heart failure, arthritis and back pain.

"Back pain, yes, chronic, it's my arthritis, Doc, it's spinal stenosis, it's discs that bulge, degenerated discs, nerve pain and yes, I take my Percocet every day. I can't function without it. Just four a day. Dr. Louise, the doctor before you, just wrote a prescription for 120 Percocet each month. And my Valium, just sixty a month for anxiety. Thank you."

She is my first. Helen is, my first chronic narcotic patient. I saw the people on lifelong opiates when I was a student. I know how this goes: the escalating doses, the never-ending cycle, the pain that gets worse over time and never seems to get better. My preceptor shrugs and sighs when I present Helen's case to her. She signs the Percocet and Valium prescriptions, since I'm not yet registered with the DEA (Drug Enforcement Agency). She, too, knows how this goes.

After Helen leaves, I pore through her records, looking for a time before the Percocet, a time before the pain, but the trail leads back fifteen years and goes cold, an unsolved crime.

I vow to find another answer for Helen. There must be another answer. Dr. Louise must not have tried hard enough. Tricyclic antidepressants. Anti-inflammatories. Physical therapy. Nerve blocks. They taught me there were other answers. I am going to find one.

After three years of residency training, I will soon be an attending at another medical school. I will pass my clinic patients along to a new intern. Several of them have died of old age or heart disease or cancer. Some are better off than when I met them in 1987; their blood pressure stable, their blood sugars in the normal range. Helen is the same. I sign the last Percocet and Valium prescriptions I will ever write for her. I sign them myself, with my own DEA number. I leave leave a note for the new resident:

> Ms. N. is stable; her medication regimen seems to be optimized. I tried every modality, every non-narcotic drug, every trick in the book, to get her off narcotics, but I failed. Please don't stop trying. But above all, please don't escalate her dose. She is on the same dose today as she was three years ago.
>
> Sadly, I consider this a triumph. At least we know she won't stop breathing on this dose.

I sign the note. I hug Helen goodbye and re-file her thick, dog-eared chart.

In the 1990s, they taught us pain was the fifth vital sign. Blood pressure, pulse, temperature, respirations—and pain. Even then, the logic eluded me. We had instruments to measure vital signs one through four; blood pressure, temperature, respirations, and pulse were objective, even if they could change rapidly and dramatically at times. But the pain scale... "Tell me how bad your pain is on a scale of zero to ten, where zero is no pain and ten is the worst pain you've ever had." This was subjective and confusing.

Still, I bought in, at least partway. I was new at the game of doctoring and didn't understand all the nuances. I didn't know how the rules might be bent, how ideas morphed with time and experience. I didn't realize that one set of data could tell three different stories, and then positions could reverse. That I might not find out times had changed until I found myself going against the current.

So, pain became the fifth vital sign. In the hospital, withholding pain medicine suddenly became the signature of a callous, uncaring doctor. The nurses called us out on allowing patients to suffer. The Joint Commission for Hospital Accreditation studied trends and cited some institutions for inadequate pain management. Patients got morphine pumps and devices for "patient-controlled analgesia." When it hurt, they hit the button, and a bolus of morphine was released into their bloodstream. On discharge, a big bottle of oral opiates was prescribed, enough to kill the pain of an entire neighborhood for weeks.

"You have to kill the pain. Get on top of it before it gets on top of you." You, the doctor, are top dog, not pain. So, be on top of it. Although the truth is big pharma was always on top. Not doctors. Not patients.

They taught us in med school to do no harm. Respect autonomy. Be altruistic. Doesn't that mean killing pain? Go ahead and pen the prescription, the pain pill prescription. A bottle of pills. A pile, a hill of pills, to kill the pain. It's safe, Big Pharma told us—the drug companies did the studies themselves. Respiratory depression? Oh, that's rare, no need for worry.

They told us to prescribe the shiny, brand-new, brand-name, slow release, newly released, but thoroughly-studied-by-the-drug-company pills. Derivatives of codeine, the ones with hydrogen and oxygen bonds, 4,5-alpha-epoxy-14-hydroxy-3methoxy-17-methylmorphinan- 6-one hydrochloride. Poetic, right? Otherwise known as Oxy. OxyContin: the long-acting form of oxycodone. What's the harm in Oxys? We all need oxygen, right? Yes, we need to breathe.

Trust us, says Big Pharma, the risk of respiratory depression is rare, very rare, in responsibly prescribed doses.

Oxys go for twenty bucks at Third and Indiana. Their short-acting cousin, oxycodone, ten bucks, but Vicodin gets just seven. Percs will only get you five. Oxys get you higher, last longer. Buyer beware, make sure you get the branded ones. What's a responsible dose when you're doing business on North Broad Street? What's the dose when, to feel an effect, you need a handful all at once?

Your money won't last long when you take the Oxys by the handful. No matter. There are cheaper forms of opiate. Your dealer knows someone who can set you up with H—yeah, that's what I mean—horse, heroin. He swears he sells pure product and clean needles. He'll help you tie the tourniquet, show you how to find the best veins. When you run out of veins, you can shoot between your toes. But the day he cuts the H with fentanyl, you won't even make it back to the corner where the guy dealing Oxys hangs out. Too bad you never got to thank him.

They taught us how to push Narcan to save the life of someone with an opiate overdose. The Narcan pulls the drug off the opiate receptors in the brain, rips the overdosing person out of the grip of death, but also out of the warm blanket and gentle dark of oblivion into ice-cold withdrawal, the harsh glare of reality and into the particular glare of the emergency room, with its bright fluorescent lights and blaring monitor alarms.

They taught us to treat pain. But now, in the E.R., it is pain or death, and we, the doctors, choose pain for our overdosing patient. We choose pain, and our patient jolts and yelps. He lunges at us, cursing and venomous. We roll our eyes, share our disdain for his self-inflicted misery. But is it really self-inflicted? Don't we have a part in this drama? Ask the patient. He might tell you it all started with the Oxys he got from his doctor.

The day Cassie died, I was at a medical conference in California. Away from my patients and my never-ending digital in-box tasks, I wasn't thinking about Cassie's symptoms or her medications, and I certainly wasn't expecting her to die. She was only twenty-six, and she didn't have a terminal illness. Or so I thought.

Cassie was sensitive and intelligent, someone with a life ahead of her. But she'd been struggling for years with physical and mental health problems after an automobile accident in her teens. She had chronic headaches, chronic abdominal and back pain, depression, anxiety, and post-traumatic stress disorder. Somewhere along the way, she'd been treated with opiates—OxyContin and oxycodone—and was on these medications when she came to me two years before her death. Despite my instinct that she was headed toward trouble with addiction, she was still on them when she died.

Early in our relationship, I raised the question with Cassie as to whether we might think about tapering her narcotics. She wasn't on a big dose, and she came regularly to her appointments. She didn't run out of pills early or ask to increase her dose. But she was also taking some Ativan, a benzodiazepine for anxiety, prescribed by her psychiatrist, and the two drugs could interact and increase the risk of respiratory depression. At this point in time, in 2012 or 2013, the opioid epidemic was already in full swing, and we were learning more all the time about the dangers of the drugs we'd once been too comfortable with.

Cassie balked at the idea of decreasing her dose. "I need it for pain!" she protested. "It's the only thing that helps me!"

I knew she was dependent. Not every patient dependent on opiates is an addict, but there's a fine line. Tolerance and withdrawal can happen with dependence, but to be addicted, there also has to be dose escalation and compulsive use of a substance despite negativ econsequences.

Cassie knew this as well as I did.

"I never take more than I'm supposed to! I never ask for refills early!" she reminded me.

Yes, that was true, but I was still worried.

I made her sign an "opioid contract," something else we were taught to do—a document promising she would take the medication only as prescribed. It stated that requests for early refills, or signs she was taking the medication improperly, or selling it on the street instead of taking it, or also using recreational drugs, or getting a prescription from someone else at the same time . . . any signs of abuse, really, that I would stop prescribing. That I could drug test her any time to make sure she was taking her medication but not recreational drugs.

For a long time, Cassie stuck to the contract. I tried to lower the dose once, and she complied, but said she was in terrible pain. I asked her to continue, to try the lower dose for another two weeks, hoping she would adjust. But instead, I got a phone call from a pharmacist, telling me Cassie had brought in a prescription for Suboxone from another doctor. Suboxone is used to help people with opiate addiction stay clean—it prevents binding of opiates to receptors in the brain that make them work. Taking both Suboxone and oxycodone would stop the oxycodone from working. Why would Cassie do this? And who gave her the Suboxone? I called the doctor listed on the prescription, but the phone rang and rang.

I called Cassie and told her what I knew. She burst into tears.

"I got the Suboxone from some pill mill clinic, because I ran out of my OxyContin too soon. I took extra because of the pain. Then I was in withdrawal! I didn't want to buy more Oxys, but I couldn't stand the withdrawal, so I got Suboxone. I didn't mean to do anything wrong! I'll never do it again!"

I wanted to trust her. I was young and smart and sensitive once, too. I identified with her.

I felt like it was my fault for trying to decrease her dose. I called her psychiatrist. Should we trust her? Should we give her another chance? We decided we should. If she doesn't get the meds from us, she might resort to street drugs, we reasoned. We can't abandon her. We kept prescribing. I kept her at the lower dose, but still, I prescribed.

We shouldn't have trusted her. Running out of medication, buying Suboxone from a pill mill, these were addict behaviors. A smart addict, but an addict. She was spiraling, and no longer had control. This likely wasn't the first time it had happened, but only the first time she got caught. She should have gone to rehab. But I let myself be lulled into complicity.

Now, a few months later, she was dead.

The coroner told me she had opiates, benzos, and alcohol in her system. It wasn't my fault, he said, if she decided to drink on top of the meds. She knew better. Yes, we all agreed. She knew. And if she took too much of her meds, or she added alcohol, that was on her, right? Right, but also wrong. We were all responsible.

We'll never know if Cassie meant to kill herself with the drugs and alcohol, or if she made a fatal mistake. We'll never know if she would have agreed to rehab, because we didn't tell her to go. Maybe it would have all gone wrong no matter what, but at least we could have tried.

"Doc, I'm going to tell you right up front. I'm a recovering addict. I'm here for antibiotics for my tooth infection. I'm not looking for pain meds."

I'm working an urgent care shift, and a forty-year-old woman sits on the exam table in room 3. She's in obvious distress, jiggling her legs to distract herself from the pain in her jaw.

She used to be a nurse on a hospital floor. She got caught taking the Oxys that were supposed to be for an end-stage cancer patient, and now she's in a recovery program. She's been clean for three years.

I offer her an injection of anti-inflammatory medication. "No opiates. Nothing addictive in it," I tell her.

"Nah, it won't even touch this," she says, as I write her penicillin prescription. "My pain tolerance is so low because of all those years of taking opiates. I've already taken the maximum dose of ibuprofen and Tylenol, and it doesn't touch the pain. So, I meditate."

"Does it work?" I ask her.

"No, not really," she replies with a wry laugh. "But it's what I've got. Every day I want to use, and every night I'm grateful I haven't used."

I like this patient. I think she's brave. I want to stay with her, hear more about her struggles, but I have another patient waiting in the next room. He's already angry because I told him I won't prescribe Percocet for his chronic back pain. I have to remember this is not all his fault.

FIVE

Brain Surgery

I hear the man's laughter in my head. His taunting voice, his ugly words. It's the laughter that lasts. It reaches into my brain with the precision of a scalpel and alters my neural chemistry, even after all these years.

It happened in the early morning hours of an overnight shift in the hospital during the third and final year of my medical residency. I was pregnant with my first child. The day preceding that shift had been an unremarkable one, spent caring for patients on the medical floors of the urban hospital where I did my Internal Medicine residency training. As a senior resident, I'd been assigned the job of House Chief that night.

The House Chief is responsible for overseeing care of patients in the medical and cardiac intensive care units, taking the role of team leader if there is a code blue, or cardiac arrest, and performing any consults for surgical patients. Routine consults to medically clear patients for surgery the next morning were to be done in the early evening, leaving only emergency consultations for the late night or early morning hours.

By 6 p.m., I'd finished end-of-the-day rounds with my daytime team, done the two pre-op consults on my list, and changed into the faded light-green surgical scrubs and sneakers that were the usual attire for overnight call. Now six months into my first pregnancy, my gravid belly had recently started blooming and could no longer be hidden, even by the loose, larger scrub tops I'd started wearing under my white coat, which now gaped open in front. I ate a quick, barely palatable meal with my colleagues in the basement cafeteria and headed up to the ICU floor to check on the situation there.

Initially, the medical intensive care and coronary care units were calm, but as the evening progressed, there were new critically ill admissions, and one of the medical ICU patients developed an unstable heart rhythm. By 11 p.m., we'd had our first code, and by 1 a.m., we'd had three—a lot even for our busy, inner-city ICU. Three calls of "Code Blue, Medical ICU" (repeated three times each for each code) and three calls of "Anesthesia Stat, Medical ICU" (also repeated three times) blared through the overhead page system, summoning all the medical and anesthesia house staff to the unit to manage an airway, compress a chest, administer epinephrine, atropine, and antiarrhythmic drugs through an IV line. By the third code, the whole team was feeling the stress of what we called a "black cloud" in the units.

After each carefully orchestrated rescue effort, the residents all scattered back to their tasks on the hospital floors or, if they were lucky, to their windowless, musty on-call rooms to catch a few minutes of sleep before the next crisis, leaving me and the ICU intern alone again with our crop of critical patients.

We managed to re-stabilize each of our three coding patients, but at about 2 a.m., I was called to evaluate a patient with chest pain on one of the general medical floors for transfer to the CCU (Coronary Care Unit).

I waited for the elevator to take me from the second floor to the seventh. When it came and the doors opened, there was one other person in the elevator, a tall, blond man I recognized as one of the second-year neurosurgery residents. He and I had never formally met, and I don't think we'd ever spoken to each other before, but I'd seen him around the hospital and knew his name was Darrell. I half smiled and nodded at him as I entered the elevator. Like me, he wore a set of surgical scrubs and a long white coat with the red hospital logo on the left arm and his name embroidered above the left breast pocket. He leaned casually against the side wall of the elevator and acknowledged me back with a barely perceptible nod.

As soon as the doors closed, though, the color of the atmosphere turned from a neutral beige to black.

"Having a bad night?" Darrell asked me. His tone was insinuating. Derisive. Or was I imagining it? Maybe it was just his accent. He had a lazy drawl. I'd heard he was from out West somewhere. He was one of the few residents at the hospital who had attended medical school that far away from Philadelphia. But neurosurgery is a highly competitive specialty, so people accept residencies wherever they can get them.

Really? I thought. *He had to have heard the codes called overhead. He knows it's not a good night.*

"It's been busy." I tried to answer evenly, calmly, though I was sure I'd detected a sneer in his voice that matched the sneer I saw on his face. It all took me by surprise, since we had no history with each other. I had no idea what he wanted from me, but there was a repellent electricity in the air in that elevator.

"Well, I'm about to make it worse," he told me. He was smiling, but not in a friendly way.

"How so?" I asked, hoping the doors would open soon.

"There's a patient on the surgery unit who needs a medical consult for a laminectomy in the morning. I hear that's your job tonight."

"A routine consult? That should have been requested during the day so I could do it while there were other people around to manage the units. We're getting slammed now, and it's already 2 a.m.," I told him, trying to keep my voice steady and quiet.

"Yeah, well, I forgot to page you earlier. I was just about to do that. The patient is scheduled for 6 a.m., and it needs to be done now." He was entirely unapologetic.

The doors to the elevator opened and I felt relief, but Darrell stepped forward quickly and blocked my way out of the elevator, standing between the two doors. The doors wouldn't close if there was a body there, but I couldn't move past him. I also realized that he'd gone up to the seventh floor with me, even though the neurology and neurosurgery units were on the fifth floor.

"Well, give me the name and room number, and I'll do it once things calm down. I'm dealing with unit transfers and codes right now. The sick patients have priority, but I'll try to get to it," I replied.

"No, it needs to be done. You can't just try to get to it." He stood in front of me, feet planted apart from each other, arms crossed.

"Listen, I need to take care of the intensive care patients. That's my priority right now. I said I would do the consult as soon as I could. I can't promise anything given what's going on right now. Let me go so I can see this chest pain patient."

I was unnerved by this point. Darrell was still blocking the door. I felt hot. I knew my voice was getting louder despite my conscious effort to modulate it.

"If you don't want to do your job, you shouldn't be a doctor," Darrell said, loudly and with a sharp edge. Now he'd moved to the side to let me pass, but he was following me into the deserted corridor outside the elevator. The fluorescent lights glared a harsh yellow against the polished white tile floor. His words echoed in the cold emptiness.

I twirled around to face him. He was too close now, his twisted, angry face too large, his body looming. My belly seemed to be all that made space between us.

"We're all busy. I said I'd do my best! Why are you being such a dick about this?" I still wasn't shouting, but I wanted to. I should have been scared, but I was angry. Or maybe I was both.

"You know what you are?" he said, still smiling. "You're a cunt. Everyone knows you're a cunt. And you're so ugly. I can't believe anyone would marry you, much less have sex with you." He was staring directly at my pregnant abdomen.

I felt as though I'd been slapped. My cheeks burned. My heartbeat pounded in my ears. I could feel my aorta twisting above my heart. I wanted to run, but running would be an admission of shame and fear. I turned and walked toward the medical unit as quickly as I could. My sneakers slapped loudly on the tile floor.

Darrell stood where he was. I heard him laugh as I entered 7 East, where I smelled the familiar mix of pine cleaner, rubbing alcohol, and stool, and was relieved to see nurses and techs sitting at the desk. I willed myself not to cry.

Pull it together. You've got to do your work, I reminded myself.

The rest of the night went by in a blur. I transferred the medical patient with chest pain to the cardiac care unit just in time for the next code blue. This time the patient didn't make it. I called the family. I filled out the death certificate and documented the resuscitation attempt. I helped the ICU intern adjust some ventilator settings. By then it was 5 a.m.

I wearily trudged to the fifth floor to do the medical consult for the neurosurgery patient. Regardless of Darrell's behavior, I didn't want the patient to suffer a delay in surgery, and there was no way I was going to let myself look like a slacker. Aside from a nurse sitting at the desk, I was the only person awake on the silent neurosurgery unit. I'm sure Darrell had been sound asleep for some time by then.

At 5:45 a.m., consult finished, I lay down on the lumpy bed in the claustrophobic little box designated as an on-call room for the intensive care units, but I didn't sleep. Darrell's words repeated in my head. *Ugly. Ugly. Ugly. I can't believe anyone would have sex with you. Cunt.* Everyone knows you're a cunt. Was I a cunt? Did people think I was nasty? I hadn't known until that night Darrell knew who I was. How would he know that people hate me? *Do people hate me? Am I ugly? Do men find me repulsive?*

Wait, no, I have a lot of friends. I've dated, mostly nice men, since I was a teenager. My husband tells me I'm beautiful every day. But maybe Darrell is right—maybe I'm disgusting, a dirty, nasty cunt.

Oh my God, snap out of it, I thought to myself. I called my husband at 6:30 a.m. and told him what happened. But I didn't tell him how frightened or ashamed I felt. I couldn't process my debasement yet. I just told him the facts. And I told him I thought it was my fault. I'd thrown the first punch by saying Darrell was "being a dick."

"I'm going to come there and kill him," Larry told me. "Telling him he's being a dick is not the same as what he did."

"No, you're not. You're not going to do anything. I'll handle it." All I really wanted was for Larry to come and fix this. But I knew I was going to have to face it myself.

"If he comes near you again," Larry replied, "I and all the other husbands of all the female residents will come there, I swear, and we will go after him."

My husband's chivalry was a nice touch, but in forty-five minutes, he would be at another hospital, doing his own work, fighting his own battles. This one was mine.

I got up, showered, and dressed. I started with the chief resident, a young man just a year ahead of me in training, my immediate superior. Ed was another tall, blond man, but unlike Darrell, he had a sunny disposition and a huge enthusiasm for medicine.

I found him in his office and recounted the events. I told Ed how Darrell had addressed me and then blocked my way in the elevator. I even told him what Darrell had called me but found myself choking on the part about my appearance and my pregnancy. I think it was difficult because I'd already internalized the words. On some level, I believed them. *Ugly. Cunt.*

It didn't matter, because Ed cut me off before I was finished.

"So, the guy got angry at you. What did you do to get him so angry?" Ed asked me.

I suddenly understood why victims often sound confused when they are questioned about what happened during an assault. I found myself, for a moment, at least, trying to answer Ed's question. I stood there with my cheeks flaming again. What *did* I do? I told Darrell he was being a dick. Yes, it *was* all my fault. No, wait—it wasn't. By then, Darrell had already provoked and intimidated me. Hadn't he? Had he?

Then I recovered.

"Never mind, Ed. I'll go to Dr. R." Dr. R was the director of the Internal Medicine residency program. Ed's reaction was because he was young and didn't know what to do. Right?

I was tired. After all, I'd been up all night caring for critically ill patients. Maybe I was too tired to think straight (although I was assumed to be thinking straight enough to take care of sick patients). If I'd been thinking straight, I should have seen it, but at the time, I hadn't—the repetition of the misogyny, the stereotyping, the re-victimization. Another white, Christian male looking at me, an outspoken, young Jewish woman with masses of thick, dark curls and an aquiline nose and seeing what he wanted to see. Surely there were policies and procedures around mistreatment and intimidation of coworkers. He wouldn't even have had to invoke sexism or anti-Semitism to advocate for me, but he was choosing not to advocate for me. Instead, he was blaming me. I definitely hadn't seen it all clearly then, but nevertheless, I knew what Ed had said to me couldn't be right.

I rounded with my team and made sure the interns knew what they needed to work on before I headed to the residency director's office. He greeted me cheerfully and invited me in. Dr. R was a rather straightlaced man in his forties, a former military officer who wore his hair in a close buzz cut as though he were still on active duty.

I sat down in the chair across from his desk. I looked around his gray, masculine office, diplomas and certificates and awards on the walls, pictures of his wife and young children on his desk. It was all so normal. But I didn't feel normal at all. I took a deep breath and began the story again, but this time I couldn't even say the word "cunt." Instead, I told him, "He called me a word that women should never be called."

"A bitch?" he asked.

"No. That would be nothing. The c-word. And then he said some other awful things about sex." I couldn't say it. "*Ugly . . . I can't believe anyone would* . . . I just couldn't say it."

"Did he put his hands on you?"

"No, but he blocked my way out of the elevator."

"So, it was just words." He put his hands on his desk. "You know, I think you should just let this go. It was late, you were both tired. People get stressed on call, and boys will be boys."

Had I heard him right? BOYS WILL BE BOYS? Was he kidding? I felt slapped again. My face burned red.

"You don't understand," I said. "This went beyond a few harsh words."

"You feel that way, but it's your word against his. It sounds like you were both angry."

So that's it, I thought. I guess I am a cunt, and people do hate me. Now I've alienated yet another man who has power over me. I got up to leave.

Dr. R's office was inside the Department of Medicine, where the chief of medicine, Dr. C, also had an office. I'd known Dr. C for a number of years. He'd been one of my professors in medical school and had changed institutions around the same time I had. As I walked past his office, I wondered if I should talk to him, but I didn't feel like I could repeat my story to yet another man. Also, he was busy, important. *Above dealing with the petty complaints of residents*, I told myself. *Besides, it probably was my fault.* I didn't want to anger my department chief.

His secretary, Nancy, was sitting at a desk outside his office. She saw me pass by and waved.

"How are you, Dr. Kaplan?"

"I've been better, Nancy."

By now, tears were leaking down my face.

Nancy looked up at me. "Oh, no. What's wrong?" she asked.

"I can't really talk about it. Just some work issues."

"Do you want to talk to Dr. C? I can make you an appointment."

I almost said no, but Nancy, a fifty-ish woman, was looking at me with a worried, maternal expression. I wanted to crawl into her lap and have her comfort me, stroke my head like a mother would with a small child. But telling the chief's secretary about another resident's behavior wasn't a good idea. I made an appointment for later that afternoon.

Dr. C had grown children, including a daughter in medical school. Maybe that's why he saw things differently. Or maybe he just had different ideas of acceptable behavior than Ed and Dr. R.

By the time I told him the story, I'd already repeated it several times. This time, I heard my voice as though it were coming from someone else, as though it were outside of me. It was flat and sad, and it sounded dispassionate. I felt far away from myself. But I said the words. All of them, including the ones voiced by Ed and Dr. R.

Dr. C listened carefully from beginning to end. By the time I'd finished, he was looking at his desk, and I wondered if he was irritated with me. Then he looked directly at me and asked, "Do you want to press charges? I'll help you if you do." I think maybe he'd looked down out of shame for his gender.

"You mean legal charges? Going to the police?"

"Yes, it's harassment. It's illegal."

I sat staring straight ahead for a minute. *Press charges? Tell this story, repeat Darrell's words in public? What if a judge blames me? I called Darrell a "dick." Maybe I should have just kept this to myself.*

"I don't think so. I'll be done here in two months. I just want to start my new job and have my baby. I don't want to be involved in court proceedings."

"Okay, then we can try to handle it internally. What do you think the consequences should be? What do you want?"

What *did* I want? I hadn't thought that through. What I wanted was to feel normal again. I wanted to walk in the hallway or enter the elevator without feeling terrorized. I wanted not to be angry. I wanted not to feel dirty and ugly and disgusting. But that wasn't something I could ask for.

"I want him gone. But maybe that's more than I want to ask for."

"We could make that a goal, if that's what you really need. I'm going to be contacting the chief of neurosurgery to discuss the situation, and I need to have a proposal for handling this," he told me.

"Okay. I don't want to ask for his dismissal, unless there are other disciplinary reports in his record. If there aren't, I want him on probation so if he does something like this again, he will be fired. And I want a report in his permanent file."

"Fair enough. He will also need to apologize to you."

"But I don't want to see him or talk to him!" I sounded like a little girl, but the idea of facing Darrell made me feel sick and hot all over again. I knew I'd likely see him at a distance in the hallways, and that I might have to speak to him about patients over the phone, but I was sure I could avoid face-to-face conversations for the rest of my time at the hospital.

"It will be a written apology," Dr. C assured me.

As I walked away from the Department of Medicine offices, I felt both relief and also uncertainty. With Dr. C on my side, I felt I could get through these last couple of months and finish my program, but there was no way to know what would actually happen. The chief of neurosurgery, whose first name was William, was known as "Wild Bill." He had a reputation for getting his way, for his temper, and for being a megalomaniac. There were no female neurosurgery residents. Darrell and the other neurosurgery residents were Bill's "boys." Who knew what someone like Wild Bill might do? He might discipline his boy, but he could just as easily decide to staunchly defend him.

Wild Bill wasn't all that wild, apparently, when it came to situations that could give his program a bad name. I don't know exactly what Dr. C said to Darrel, but I imagine the idea of a lawsuit in the neurosurgery department, especially a sexual harassment lawsuit, didn't seem like a good thing.

The next afternoon, I answered a page to an unfamiliar extension. "Dr. Kaplan," I answered the phone.

"This is Dr. B, the chief of neurosurgery." Wild Bill himself was on the phone.

"Hello, Dr. B," I said. I sat at one of the charting workstations on a medical floor, my heart pounding, examining a bitten fingernail to distract myself.

"I spoke with Dr. C. I want to personally apologize for my resident's behavior."

"Well, thanks, but you're not responsible for his behavior."

"Well, I am, in a way. I don't want trouble amongst our residents."

By the time our phone conversation ended, I was assured that my terms were being met. I thanked Dr. B, feeling pleasantly surprised, but also wondering if I was being tricked.

"Thank you for not taking this further," he said, as he ended the conversation.

After I hung up, I felt a little sick. *"Thank you for not taking this further."* That's what he cared about. He probably thought I was a crazy woman, trying to make trouble for one of the boys. He was just doing damage control. Maybe I should have pressed charges.

In the following weeks, I told some of my friends what had happened. The women were horrified, realizing it could happen to any of us. My male friends, who tended to be the more feminist of the men, were outraged and incensed that members of their gender were making all men look bad. Everyone agreed that Ed and Dr. R had mismanaged the event. Many of the men said they'd like to beat Darrell up. But I knew that fighting emotional violence with physical violence wasn't a viable option. It wouldn't give the message I wanted to give.

One friend, a resident in a different surgical specialty, and one of the few women in the whole surgery department, pulled me aside.

"Do you know Darrell's story?" Anne asked me.

"No, I don't know anything about him."

"Well, he's married to the daughter of a prominent neurosurgeon in New Mexico. Someone who is good friends with Wild Bill. That's the only reason he's here. Everyone says he couldn't get into any other neurosurgery program because of negative evaluations in medical school. Wild Bill was the only one who would take him."

Great. The Old Boys' Network, ignoring red flags and pushing a doctor through, granting him power over patients and over those training under him. Darrell, like all neurosurgeons, worked on patients at some of their most vulnerable moments, when they needed surgery on their brains or spinal cords, and alongside fellow physicians at stressful, critical moments. It was a chilling revelation.

A few days later, a letter from Darrell appeared in my staff mailbox.

> *Dear Dr. Kaplan,*
>
> *I'm writing this apology to you for the encounter we had last week. I'm sorry I was rude, but we both know it's just as much your fault. But now I'm on probation because of you, and I had to write this apology.*
>
> *Dr. Darrell _____.*

An apology that doesn't apologize. What did I expect? I ripped it up, threw it out, and left it at that. I didn't have the heart, or the energy, to bring it to Dr. C or Wild Bill. I was afraid to push the issue for fear they would take away what had been given. Anyway, there was still a part of me that believed what Darrell had written.

I had no more to do with Darrell. I finished my residency. I started a new job at a different institution. I had a baby coming. I tried not to think about him, and most of the time I succeeded. But there were the moments of self-doubt when his voice crept into my head. *Had I provoked him? Did people hate me? Was I ugly? Disgusting? A cunt?* Darrell hadn't needed to do neurosurgery on me to cause changes in my brain.

Anne, the surgery resident, called me sometime about a month after I finished the program—a short while before my baby was due.

"I thought you'd want to know. Darrell was thrown out of the neurosurgery program."

"Really? You're serious?"

"Yeah, he was verbally abusive to a nurse in the O.R., and he threw scissors at her. He was on probation, so they axed him. I think Wild Bill had given up on him even before that. I heard he wasn't a very good resident."

I should have known that I wasn't going to be the last person to be abused by Darrell. I'm sure I wasn't the first, but it was probably easier for whomever came before me to keep it to herself. Speaking up hadn't been easy and getting someone to listen had been even harder. I wished I'd pushed to have him dismissed. It could have saved that poor nurse. But it took this second episode to make me believe he deserved it, that it really was *him* and not me.

It's been thirty years now. And it's taken all this time for me to understand what happened that night with Darrell. The misogyny and xenophobia, the opinion of me as a woman and as a professional that Darrell thought he had a right to voice. I'm not the standard American ideal of beauty—I'm not tall and blonde with an upturned nose, but rather a woman with thick, dark curls, an aquiline nose, a Semitic appearance that had offended his sensibilities. A woman doing a man's job. A woman saying no to him.

It still haunts me. Darrell's sneer, his laugh floating down the hallway toward 7 East after he'd called me a cunt and ugly and had questioned why anyone would impregnate me. His taunting tone. His body blocking my way out of the elevator, following me down a deserted hallway in the early hours of the morning.

During the Brett Kavanaugh hearings, Senator Patrick Leahy asked Dr. Christine Blasey Ford what the strongest memory she had of her assault was.

She replied, "Indelible in the hippocampus is the laughter . . . having fun at my expense."

When I heard Blasey Ford's reply, my chest tightened in visceral agreement. What bothers me the most is that I had the sense Darrell enjoyed our encounter. He left it laughing. I left it traumatized, wounded, and eventually scarred.

Maybe I'd been a fool all along. It's not as though I'd never encountered sexism in my training before Darrell came along. In fact, my anatomy professor in my first year of medical school had included occasional pictures of naked women in his lecture slide decks to "amuse" the male students, and during a plastic surgery rotation in my third year of med school, a male resident had asked if I wanted a free breast augmentation. During my internship, the male chief residents had joked that all the female residents should have to wear red when we had our periods, to reassure the male residents that we weren't pregnant since pregnancies and maternity leave (which was unpaid) would mess up the call schedule.

Like all the other women, I tried to ignore or laugh off these incidents, since they were perpetrated by men who had power over me, and complaining could have jeopardized my career. When male patients or colleagues paid me unwanted attention, I simply removed myself from the situation as quickly as possible. Up until my encounter with Darrell, avoidance had worked for me, but avoidance came with a price. Back then, I think all women in medicine paid the price of questioning our perceptions and pushing down our feelings. We didn't have much recourse.

Thankfully, now that women occupy more than fifty percent of medical school classes in the U.S., there is some recourse. But the change is glacially, agonizingly slow. Women in healthcare still struggle against a system that pays women considerably less for doing the same work and has few women in leadership positions. Frighteningly, the Old Boys Network still has its hold over medicine. With mostly male leaders, micro-aggressions are still mostly tolerated, while many macro-aggressions go unreported or unpunished. Women continue to experience minimization of their concerns at best, and retribution at worst, when they report harassment. We continue to fear for our reputations and livelihoods. To me, it is amazing that the field of healthcare, a field that is, in theory, held to higher standards of ethics and behavior, a discipline which is well aware of the lasting, devastating effects of trauma, both physical and emotional, is so resistant to change.

Still, at least sexual harassment is now being discussed in academic institutions and hospital systems, and most of these entities have developed processes for reporting and investigating incidents. Blatant sexual harassment against students, trainees, and employees is no longer tolerated, at least in academic environments. Health care had its own campaign, #Time'sUpHealthcare, part of the larger Time's Up initiative, founded by Hollywood celebrities to support workers in all industries in speaking up about sexual assault and harassment. And yes, time has been up for years, but that doesn't mean my students and residents will never again encounter someone like Darrell among their colleagues.

If Darrell ever thinks of me, I imagine it is as "one of the cunts who ruined my career." I think of Darrell all too often, more than I really want to admit.

I thought of him last year when my daughter's beautiful friend from Singapore, the one with the silky, dark locks and the smooth, golden skin, sat tearfully in my kitchen, relating how a young man she'd gone out with told her she wasn't his type; she was only a three or four on a scale of ten because she wasn't white and she wasn't thin enough.

I thought about him when an administrator at my last job sat and stared me down with icy eyes that looked like those of a Siberian husky, arms folded and legs spread wide, telling me, "Your problem is you spend too much time with patients." Code for "your problem is you're female."

I thought about him when a forty-five-year-old female patient with gonorrhea told me that her husband was sleeping with other women because she was no longer pretty enough for him.

I thought about him when white supremacists ran over Heather Heyer in Charlottesville in 2017 and when Jews were gunned down in a synagogue in Pittsburgh in 2018. Not that what he did to me came anywhere close to these heinous crimes, but because the dehumanization and the sheer hatred he demonstrated are on the same continuum of evil.

I looked Darrell up after watching the Kavanaugh hearings. I know exactly what made me do it. It was Christine Blasey Ford's description of the laughter that came from Kavanaugh and his friend after the assault. What I don't know is why I hadn't looked him up sooner. I think it may have been because I feared confirmation of his existence would make me feel unsafe.

I hoped had he wasn't practicing medicine. But he is. In a southern state. He's not a neurosurgeon. I suppose he couldn't get into another neurosurgery program. But it's almost worse. He's an anesthesiologist. He's the person who is supposed to care about his patients' pain and to watch over their safety while the surgeon is trying to fix whatever is broken inside. He is alone in rooms with unconscious people. Maybe unconscious women. He can say things about them while they're asleep. He can touch them however he wants if nobody else is looking.

There were only a few patient reviews of Darrell online. They were all bad. One patient said he was arrogant, rude, and uncaring. Another said he would never return to this doctor because he woke up in the middle of his surgery. To be fair, online reviews are often skewed to the negative, but these were extreme.

Would anything be different if I'd pressed charges? Would he have lost his license?

Probably not, and even if he did, he likely would have gotten it back quickly. It was 1990, and it was my word versus his. It had been "only words." Sticks and stones. But those words have haunted me for thirty years. He took part of my confidence, a piece of what I'd always believed—that I was a beautiful, smart, powerful woman—and "put me in my place." *Just an ugly cunt.*

I recently read an article about the difference between calling a man a dick and calling a woman a cunt. It was written by a man. He essentially posited that to say a man is being a dick is to say he is a jerk, being mean, or unpleasant. But nobody says a woman is being a cunt. They say she is a cunt, and the word "cunt" is said by dictionary.com to be one of the strongest words in the English language—an obscene word of disparagement. It reduces a woman to genitalia and denounces her genitalia as offensive. In 1979, Andrea Dworkin described the word as reducing women to "the one essential—'cunt: our essence...our offence.'"

If you call me a bitch—it means I'm an angry woman and, while disparaging, does not offend me in the same way. Even call me a twat, which I would interpret as saying I'm an idiot. But if you call me a cunt, you are taking my entire gender down with me, reducing us all to filth.

Trauma is Greek for wound. Wounds turn to scars—the memory of the wound, the remnants of trauma.

There will always be moments now when I hear Darrell's voice, see his sneer, remember that laughter. He and I both knew he could have hurt me worse if he'd wanted to, but in his eyes, I wasn't even worth the effort.

SIX

Dancing with Death

My dress is bright red. It is Lycra, shiny, its bodice clinging close to my upper body. The skirt, though not tight, is too short for my comfort, and ends in a handkerchief hemline. When I twirl, it flares out dramatically Underneath the skirt I wear black fishnet pantyhose. My shoes are gold with a stiletto heel and an ankle strap; the sole is soft leather, specially constructed for the smooth wood floor.

If I'd known this would be the costume for the Latin number Larry and I would be performing at the Showcase for the School of Ballroom and Latin Dance, perhaps I would have advocated for a foxtrot or a West Coast swing instead. It had been the idea of our instructors, Scott and Christina, to perform a *paso doble*, a Latin salsa-type dance. Scott had acted as choreographer, and Christina had come up with the costumes. Of course, Larry's outfit was much more subdued— black pants and vest with a white shirt. Christina had wanted the red Lycra and the fishnets, and I hadn't want to hurt her feelings by rejecting her design.

Lest anyone believe that Larry and I are proficient dancers on this night, let me dispel that notion right away. We'd been taking dance lessons for only a couple of years, and our skills were quite mediocre. We get the steps right, usually. I'm graceful enough, after years of ballet lessons as a child and teen, but don't have the confidence to throw in dramatic hand or head motions, so my style is lacking. For Larry's part, he never quite got the hang of "Latin hips," so he's a little stiff on the dance floor. Together, we get most of the steps, but our teamwork needs ongoing attention.

No matter our level, all the students are encouraged to perform once a year, and the School of Ballroom and Latin Dance rents out the largest ballroom at the Union League Club of Philadelphia, a venerable institution founded as a patriotic society in 1862. Larry and I call it the "Bastion of Old White Men" as the hallways are lined with portraits of its original white male members; women and people of color were not allowed in the Union League until the late Twentieth Century. Nevertheless, the ballroom is grand, and the dance floor massive. Families and friends of those of us performing buy tickets and come to eat dinner, watch the show, and dance during open dance numbers between performances.

Larry and I are third on the schedule. We watch the first couple glide by in formal wear, engaged in a foxtrot, before we are entertained by a rousing jitterbug from a woman in a flapper dress and a man in high-rise cuffed trousers. When our number is announced, we arrange ourselves in the center of the dance floor with our right hips jutted out and our left knees flexed a bit. The music starts and our body memory kicks in. We flub a double turn but manage to get back on the right foot and proceed. Our enthusiastic audience (with rather low standards, apparently) claps wildly as Larry dips me at the end, my leg high in the air, showing plenty of fishnet-covered thigh.

Later, we will watch the video and laugh at our mistakes and our sometimes-awkward movements. No harm; the Showcase is always good fun. But for now, we scamper back to our seats to catch our breath.

The host announces an open dance Viennese waltz, and a stately older couple, perhaps late seventies, tall and lean and white-haired, begins to dance. I notice how beautifully the woman holds her head, the straight line of her back, and how firmly her partner (I assume her husband) guides her. He is a strong lead, something Larry is working on, but has not yet mastered. They move together as one, and it appears effortless. I muse at the grace and lightness of their steps. And then, suddenly, the man drops to the ground. It happens so quickly and so silently that I almost wonder if I've imagined it. But no, he is lying on the dance floor catty-corner to our table, and there is now a flurry of activity around him, as his partner stands stock-still, the serene tilt of her head now gone, her hands covering her mouth and her eyes wide.

Larry, who is busy chatting with the man to his right, hasn't noticed this spectacle.

Without thinking or saying a word, I leap up from the table and run across the floor. Another guest is leaning over the fallen gentleman, who is unconscious.

"He's breathing!" I hear her say hopefully. But I look down, and his face is pallid, grayish, and he makes a tiny gasping noise that I recognize as agonal breathing, a reflex indicating that the brain is not getting oxygen, a sign that he is near death, most likely from cardiac arrest or massive stroke. I kneel beside him, yelling

"Someone call 911," as I check his pulse. Absent. I tilt his head back to give a rescue breath and look around to see if someone else appears capable of performing CPR (cardiopulmonary resuscitation).

A crowd has now gathered, and every mouth around me is agape, but Larry has seen the spectacle and is on his way across the floor. I give another breath and then straddle the man to begin chest compressions. Larry moves in wordlessly, and we embark on two-rescuer CPR. Larry fortunately has the presence of mind to turn to a man next to him and bark, "Go to security and ask if they have a defibrillator." Meanwhile, someone announces that they've alerted 911 and the EMTs (emergency medical technicians) are on the way.

I can't accurately say how long all this takes. Time is suspended. After four or five cycles of compressions, my arms ache, and Larry and I switch places. Then an automatic external defibrillator (AED) appears, and Larry rips the man's already-ruined dress shirt off and attaches the pads to his chest. We both move away enough that we are no longer touching him, and I watch the defibrillator box register a wavy line.

"V-fib," the machine announces. "Proceed to shock."

"Clear," I yell and push the red button. The unconscious man jolts.

Larry checks for a pulse while I watch the monitor. "No pulse. Resume CPR."

I give a breath, and he compresses. We move back again.

"V-fib," the machine announces again. "Proceed to shock." I silently wish for a hospital crash cart, for epinephrine and atropine and an IV to improve the chance of survival, but all we have is the AED.

"Clear," I yell, and push the red button again. Another jolt, and still no pulse. We repeat our ministrations.

It's the fourth shock, or maybe the fifth, that finally works. There's a spike on the monitor afterward, indicating a heartbeat. Then another, and another.

"We've got a rhythm," I exclaim.

Larry cranes his neck to see the monitor. "Looks like a normal rhythm!" he says excitedly.

I feel the carotid artery for a pulse, and there it is, weak but present, and I can see the chest rise as he takes a shallow breath.

How long has it been? A minute? An hour? No, something in between, maybe fifteen minutes or twenty? Were our compressions enough to perfuse his brain? And where in hell is the ambulance? Where are the EMTs?

As though by divination, two EMTs arrive just at that moment, pushing a stretcher, crash box in hand. Larry begins to speak, explaining what transpired, how many cycles of CPR, how many shocks, while one of the EMTs checks vital signs and starts an IV line. I stand up from my kneeling position on the floor and register the group standing around us, some of whom, now that the extreme situation is over, are drifting back to their tables. The man's dance partner still stands, silently watching, seemingly frozen in place.

"Oh, my God, are you his..."

"His wife," she says. I see her lip tremble and put out my arms in time for her to collapse into them.

"It's okay, they're stabilizing him," I tell her. I know it isn't really okay. The likelihood of someone surviving an out-of-hospital cardiac arrest is less than ten percent, even with bystander intervention. Still it is as "okay" as it possibly can be, given the circumstances.

I turn to the EMT who is writing down what Larry tells him. "Where will you be taking him?"

"Closest E.R. is Graduate Hospital," he replies.

"And his wife, will you take her as well?"

"No, we can't—we'll need space for all the equipment and both of us to work on him.

We have a driver out there in the ambulance. She'll have to come separately."

"Are you here with anyone else?" I ask her.

"No," she tells me, beginning to cry.

"Okay, we're going to take you there." I know Larry will agree, so I don't hesitate. "You need a coat. It's very cold out. I'm going to get mine and meet you right by that door." I point to the main entrance to the ballroom.

She nods silently as she watches the EMTs transfer her husband, still unconscious, now hooked up to IV fluids and a heart monitor, oxygen tubing in his nose, to the stretcher. They start moving the stretcher toward the door. She inhales sharply and turns to get her coat.

Larry goes to get our car from the parking garage, and I lead the woman, who is now teary and limp, down the steps and out to the street. Graduate Hospital, which will close as a full-service hospital just a year later, in 2007, is only six blocks away, but the traffic makes the trip slow and plodding.

The time allows us to introduce ourselves. She is Mrs. P. We tell her we are physicians and try to calm and reassure her. She thanks us repeatedly and we demur.

"It's just what we automatically do," we say.

In fact, it was completely automatic. We'd been so thoroughly trained to recognize emergencies, to step in and take charge, to follow the protocols, that we couldn't imagine doing otherwise. It was as though the flow chart for emergency procedure appeared in front of our eyes, and we carried out the steps without thinking.

There'd been other times I'd needed to perform CPR outside the hospital. There was the woman who'd collapsed right in front of me in the Philadelphia airport. I was holding my year-old son and had to hand him over to an airline agent while I tried to resuscitate her. Two years later, eight and a half months pregnant with my daughter, I entered a friend's apartment building to find a woman screaming for help in the lobby. Her husband had been pulseless on the floor for more than five minutes; she didn't know how to do CPR. I'm pretty certain he was beyond help by the time I started resuscitation. As far as the woman in the airport, I never found out what happened, but my best guess is she didn't make it.

Arriving at the E.R., we park in the emergency lot and usher Mrs. P through the E.R. doors. It is bracingly cold outside; I haven't taken the time to close my coat, but I clutch the front panels together to stay warm. I haven't been in Graduate's

E.R. for over twenty years at that point, but, as a medical student, I'd done part of my general surgery rotation at Graduate, and I feel a spark of recognition even all these years later. I take Mrs. P's arm and lead her to the reception desk.

"This is Mrs. P. Her husband was brought in by ambulance probably just a few minutes ago," I tell the nurse.

"Oh, yes, just a moment. I'm going to go get the doctor for you," she replies.

We sit on beige vinyl chairs in the stark and empty waiting room. She holds herself stiffly, her face now stoic. I wonder fleetingly how it would feel to be waiting to hear if *my* husband, the man who, not an hour earlier, was my dance partner, gliding me across a shiny wood floor in a ballroom, is alive. Then I shake off the thought.

"Mrs. P?" A male voice reaches us, followed by the man it belongs to, a stocky man with tired eyes and graying temples in green surgical scrubs and a white coat. "I'm Dr. Smith. Your husband is stable. It looks like he's had a heart attack, and the cardiologist is in with him right now. They want to take him to the cardiac catheterization lab. You know, he was really lucky. Most people who have a cardiac arrest like that don't even make it to the hospital alive."

"Well, these are the people who saved his life," she tells him, gesturing to me and Larry. I feel myself flush. I'm not yet sure that he was saved. He could die in the cath lab, or maybe he is already brain-damaged from loss of oxygen.

"Why don't you go join your husband," Dr. Smith says. "I'll get some information from these folks."

"Yes, please," she answers. She thanks us again.

Before she walks through the door to the clinical area, Larry slips her his card. "Let us know if there's anything we can do for you." And then she is gone.

Larry and I stand facing Dr. Smith.

"So what exactly were you all doing when Mr. P collapsed?" Dr. Smith asks. I notice he is directing his question to Larry. He makes no eye contact with me and seems to be subtly smirking.

"Dancing," says Larry.

"Dancing," repeats Dr. Smith, skeptically. "And how is it that you people know how to do CPR?" Now he looks at me. In fact, he looks me up and down. I glance down at my feet and see the gold stiletto heels and it hits me.

I am standing in an E.R. waiting room, my coat hanging open, in a red Lycra minidress and fishnet stockings. I had done CPR in a red Lycra mini dress and fishnet stockings. At a ballroom dance showcase, nobody would think twice about my attire, but in the E.R., it's…well…incongruous. I was so intent on handling Mr. P's emergency that I hadn't thought for a second about what I wore, or how we (well, mostly *I*) must look standing there.

"Well, actually," I blurt, "we're doctors. I know we look kind of strange, but we were in the middle of a dance performance, and the whole thing happened right after we finished our salsa dance, and…" My voice trails off.

I imagine he thinks we are either crazy or we are lying. But really, who cares? Truth really is stranger than fiction, I think to myself. Dr. Smith works in an E.R. He should know that by now. What difference does it make anyway? What if he thinks I'm a hooker? What if he thinks I was "entertaining" Mr. P when he had his cardiac arrest? What difference does any of it make?

"Okay, if there's nothing else you need to know, we're going to go," Larry says, and we head for the door.

We return to the dance showcase. We've left our street clothes there, at the Union League Club. Besides, there are two more hours of performances scheduled, and we think we want to watch. But when we get back there, I can't keep my mind off Mr. P. What is going to happen to him? Is Mrs. P okay there by herself, waiting for her husband to come out of the cath lab?

Strangely, when we enter the ballroom, a few people greet us, but nobody comments on Mr. P's collapse or asks about the resuscitation. Everyone is busy eating and drinking, talking about the dancers, watching the performances. They've all moved on already, but I haven't. I look at Larry and we lock eyes.

"I don't want to stay," I tell him quietly.

"Neither do I," he says. "I can't get back into it. Let's go home."

We don't talk about it anymore. There isn't anything to say; we both just need to process the events of the night. Like so many times our pagers went off during family dinners or in the middle of sleep, we were pulled abruptly out of the non-medical part of our lives and into someone else's drama, into their intimacies, their complications, their tragedies and traumas, their near misses. And once you are pulled in, it isn't always easy to walk back out. Your mind lingers in the whys and the what-ifs, the realization that, someday, this could be your own tragedy or trauma or, if you're lucky, your own near-miss. It was not my life that was altered that evening. Our lives remain, on the outside, unchanged, but everything looks a little different on the inside.

We get a call from Mrs. P a few days later. Mr. P, she tells us, has survived not only the catheterization, but also a subsequent triple bypass surgery. He's still recovering in the hospital, but she expects the doctors to discharge him in the next day or two. His brain, she says, seems unharmed. It's almost miraculous. Completely against the odds.

A few months will go by, and Larry and I will stop going to the School of Ballroom and Latin Dance, our lessons becoming a casualty of our too-busy lives and the priorities we set. We will have learned enough to dance at Bar Mitzvahs and weddings, to pull off a rhumba or a double-step, though the choreography and rhythm never become true second nature.

After the Showcase, whenever Larry and I dance, I will think of Mr. and Mrs. P. I will envision their graceful teamwork. I will relive the split second in which Mr. P stopped being Mrs. P's graceful dance partner, and the moments in which he almost died. I will wonder if they ever had the chance to waltz again.

SEVEN

Dream Logic

In the moments when you were dying, I was eighty miles away, examining a young woman's swollen ankle in a sterile, blue-white exam room under glaring fluorescent lights. Her ankle was improving, reassuring me that the antibiotics I'd prescribed days earlier were working. She was my only patient that morning, the morning of Christmas Eve, 1990.

In my mind, I see your bedroom, the room in which you died on that morning. There are shafts of gray light auguring light snow peeking through the slats of the vertical blinds on the windows flanking the dark wood headboard. The walls and carpet are a tasteful, unobtrusive ecru. The headboard is against the far wall, the matching bureau to the right of the door.

I see you waking in your place on the left side of the bed, your side, with its two pillows covered in lilac-colored pillowcases. I see the crumpled lilac sheets and patterned pastel comforter over your lower body as you sit up in your white cotton nightgown, your short, dark curls wild around your face. But the image stops there.

I can't see your expression. I can't hear the words Dad told me you spoke,

"Call 911, I'm dying." *I can't envision the gestures you might have made. Did you hold your chest, fist to sternum, in the universal sign for chest pain? Did you clutch your head or neck? Did your eyes go wide with fear or surprise?*

I can't see you slump back on the lilac pillows, pulseless and pallid, though I imagine this is what happened.

I imagine this part only in words. I find the words and write them down, but the images don't appear in my mind's eye. Did Dad believe your words? Did he pick up the phone while you still had blood pulsing through your arteries? He wouldn't have tried to breathe life back into you, or press on your chest, trying to keep your heart in motion, because he didn't know how to perform CPR.

Weeks later, when I asked for details, he told me, "I don't remember."

I try to see, to hear, to know, but I will never know. I wasn't there. I was in a cold, glaring blue-white room, examining a young woman's swollen ankle. She was fine, but you weren't. You were leaving the world. Leaving me.

My mother's sudden death has been one of the defining moments in my life. She was sixty-two years old and not sick, had no medical problems except high blood pressure, for which she took a medication. I was thirty, a new doctor, a new mother. I remember the phone call with my father in a distorted, slowed-down, time-release way. "Your mother has had a massive heart attack." Right after the words "heart attack," I knew she was dead, and I handed the phone to my husband, Larry, who had stood next to me when I took the call.

I'd headed home after seeing only one patient in the medical office where Larry and I worked because it was the beginning of a holiday. Only urgent visits had been scheduled. Anita, the secretary Larry and I shared, who referred to us as Mrs. Dr. Kaplan and Mr. Dr. Kaplan, had tracked me down after my father called the office. Anita said, "Your father told me it wasn't an emergency. But if he called here on a holiday, I thought it must be important." So, she called me at home.

After I found out my mother was dead, I said to my dad, "Why did you tell Anita it wasn't an emergency?" Then I realized it wasn't. She was already dead.

I think of defining moments as the ones that I remember, no matter how long ago they occurred, as though they happened yesterday, or this morning, or five minutes ago. They are the moments that took my breath--bowling balls hitting my solar plexus. Moments for which I have crystal-clear recall of my surroundings and activities years after the fact: JFK's assassination, 9/11, my mother's death.

I was only three-years-old when JFK was shot, yet I remember the events, or think I do, as they occurred in my child's world. I was playing in my bedroom, sitting on the floor near my iron trundle bed. Across the hall, my mother folded laundry while she watched our black-and-white RCA television set with the rabbit-ear antenna. I heard a sudden gasp, and then my mother crying. Sobbing. That's how I remember it.

I was afraid to move, afraid to go into her room. But after some unclear amount of time, she came to me and explained that the president had died. I still didn't understand why she was crying. We didn't know the president.

On the morning of September 11, 2001, I was in another exam room, this one decorated in the dark wood and mauve textiles favored by designers of doctors' offices at the time—a palette intended to appear nonthreatening, to calm anxious patients. I was in the middle of performing a physical exam when my nurse knocked and summoned me out of the room. She told me that planes had hit the Twin Towers in Manhattan, that possibly something had also happened in Washington, D.C. She'd heard this on the radio. Nobody knew what it all meant yet.

The phone in my office started ringing wildly in the next few minutes. My children's schools, telling me they were safe. I could pick them up early if I chose to. My husband, asking if I knew, if I was okay. A friend who could not reach her sister in Manhattan.

The radio chattered on with new but unconfirmed information. It felt as though the world was experiencing a sandstorm. Everyone was blinded in this storm. We waited for the wind to stop so we could assess the damage, but the gusts blew for days.

The gusts from my mother's death lasted years for me. My mother knew my first child, Max, for only three months. He'd entered the world that September. His birth had been chaotic, by emergency caesarian section, a sudden turn in the middle of a difficult labor. Doctors and nurses had yelled commands, pulled him out of me in a sterile surgical field. I was numb from the waist down.

After an initial surge of fear, I was also emotionally numb.

Max spent a week in the neonatal intensive care unit after turning blue in the nursery the night of his birth, a week during which I remained insensate until we were finally released from the hospital.

At home, Max was an unusually alert, almost vigilant baby. He suffered from what we called "colic" then, screaming for hours from the late afternoon into the evening for the first few months of his life. Now my pediatrician friends say that he probably had acid reflux; they give babies antacid for this and say it works wonders. Back then, all we could do was walk the floors with him and wait for time to pass.

I was a weepy, frightened, shell-shocked mother in those first months, though I could look competent when necessary. I was too insecure to nurse Max in front of people. I didn't sleep at night, afraid he would stop breathing again. I didn't know what to do with an infant who stared at me wide-eyed, as though waiting for something to happen, whenever he was awake. I carried him in a Snugli and read the *New York Times* aloud to him in a high-pitched, hysterical tone. I often wanted to give him back, but there was no return policy.

My mother, though, was in love with Max from the minute she first saw him. She told me from the beginning that he was extraordinary.

"I'm not just saying that because he's my grandson. He's special. He's brilliant." My mother was a child psychologist. I wanted to believe that she actually knew something that no one else did, but I had no evidence. As adorable as my blond-mohawked, blue-eyed baby was, I worried that the colic and his hypoxic episode in the hospital foretold some defect, some impending disaster.

At the time my mother died, the colic was just starting to dissipate. I was back at work as a doctor and assistant professor at one of the area medical schools, regaining my footing in the world, and

I was developing some confidence in my parenting. I finally felt bonded to my baby. I believed my world was safe again.

My mother's death sent me hurtling back into the stratosphere. If she could suddenly drop dead, then anything and everything catastrophic was possible at any moment.

During the time I spent with my father in New Jersey, I learned he was not at all certain that my mother had died from a heart attack. He only knew she had told him she was dying. It could have been her heart, or it could have been a stroke, or a ruptured aneurysm. My father chose not to get an autopsy. I'll never know what really happened. I suppose it doesn't matter, except to quiet my mind.

Sometimes I have macabre fantasies: that she died by suicide and my father was covering it up. I have even wondered if my father killed her. But I don't believe my own imaginings. My father was an extremely gentle and honest person. I don't believe he was a murderer. I don't believe it was his fault. It's just difficult to accept an explanation that explains nothing.

After my mother's funeral and the ritual week of Jewish mourning, I came back to my home in Philadelphia. I returned to my routine of seeing patients, teaching, caring for my baby, making dinners, being with my husband. I pushed through. I pretended nothing had changed. But my world felt unsafe. Soon I lived in a "new normal" life, a shaky equilibrium—something that looked like recovery, though it was really just a holding pattern.

The first dream I had about you made me wonder if I was crazy or some kind of misguided psychic. The dream came in October, when Max was just a little more than a year old. You visited me from the world of the dead. I couldn't see you, but I could hear you. I knew you were there. A disembodied spirit. You returned because you wanted Max with you in the world of the dead. Somehow, that wasn't unreasonable in the dream, but it wasn't acceptable to me, and I argued with you. I said you couldn't have him, and you told me I didn't have a choice. This was as far as our negotiation went.

I woke with a start out of that dream to the insistent ringing of the phone. It was 6:30 a.m., and my husband's father was on the other end. Just an hour earlier, Larry's sister had found her two-month-old son, Andrew, cold and blue in his crib. Later it was determined that he'd died from sudden infant death syndrome.

I told no one about my dream. I secretly felt Andrew's death was my fault. My mother had wanted Max, and I wouldn't give him up to her. Awake, I imagined I'd somehow won the argument with my mother in the dream, and she'd taken our nephew instead. There was no logic to these thoughts. My dream logic was so powerful, it drove my waking thoughts.

The weekend before my mother died, she asked me for something, and I refused her.

Larry, Max, and I were visiting with Larry's parents in Central New Jersey, and my parents had joined us all at their home on Sunday afternoon. When it was time for my parents to leave, Max was napping in his Pack 'n Play crib.

"Could I wake him, just for a moment, to say goodbye?" my mother asked me. "Mom, no! Nobody wakes a sleeping baby!" I replied.

"Just for a minute. He'll go back to sleep."

"No. He'll be up if you wake him." The truth was, I needed the break. I was thinking of myself.

Instead, she snuck into the room where he slept, and watched him sleep for a minute. Then she left. It was the last time I saw my mother alive, and the last time my mother saw my son.

She'd wanted to say goodbye. "Goodbye" is a strong word. Why not "good night?" Had she known something? *Did you, Mom? Did you know something then? Should I have known something?*

In my first days at home after Max's birth, my mother tried to help me adjust, to relax into motherhood, to get over my fears. She came to Philly and stayed for a few days when he was just a couple of weeks old. She held him while I showered. She helped with laundry and cooking while I nursed him. She helped me find a nanny to give me respite for a few hours a day until I went back to work, and then to care for Max while I was at work. Then she left abruptly, telling me I needed to "get back" to my life. I was still a mess. I wasn't ready for her to leave.

"You need to go back to work," she told me. "You'll feel better, more normal, when you do. Don't get caught in the kiddie coop like I did."

Don't get caught in the kiddie coop? That wasn't going to happen. I was going back to work three days a week after six weeks of maternity leave. I'd worked hard for my M.D. and had given up three years of sleep and leisure to do my medical residency. That was not all going to waste.

I agreed with her that I needed to go back to work. Nevertheless, I took her comment as a rejection. Had she not loved me and my brother when we were babies? Had she resented caring for us when we were little?

Now, I understand. She'd loved us every bit as much as I love my children, but she'd also wanted a career. When we were babies, she hadn't had that choice. She had a master's degree in education, but she, like all the other white, suburban mothers in the early1960s, was expected to stay home with her children. She had taught junior high school in Evanston, Illinois, before she married my father, but the income from teaching was not enough to justify a woman married to an educated, professional man to continue working. Besides, she later told me, it was not a stimulating job, not one that gave her the satisfaction she needed from the work world.

When I was three years old, she returned to school to pursue her doctorate in psychology. Twice a week for two years, she drove over an hour to attend classes at Rutgers University. When she was at school, we had a babysitter—a stout, elderly woman from our neighborhood named Mrs. Bosch. I'm sure my mother was ostracized by some in the community for her ambitions and criticized for leaving her children for entire days, which was highly unusual then. Regardless, my brother, Bob, and I loved Mrs. Bosch. My memories of those days were good ones. I don't remember feeling traumatized by my mother's time away from me.

I remember Mrs. Bosch sitting at the round, white Formica kitchen table with us as we ate our sandwiches and drank our milk at lunchtime. After lunch, on nice days, we took a walk into the little downtown of Somerville, New Jersey. Mrs. Bosch took us to the Gaston Street Bakery, where we each got a cupcake, or to the five-and-dime where she bought us each a five-pack of Charms lollipops. Each pack had a cherry, orange, grape, lemon, and lime pop, each wrapped in a plastic wrapper of the corresponding color, held together with clear tape wrapped around their smooth, white, perfectly rounded sticks. The lollipops, usually purchased on Thursdays, were meant to last us until Mrs. Bosch's next visit—one each day from Thursday until the following Tuesday.

Mrs. Bosch also repaired our clothing, sewing on buttons and stitching seams, and more importantly, our stuffed animals. Bob, twenty months older than me, had a light-brown stuffed dog with floppy ears named Cocoa, because the color resembled that of milky hot chocolate. I had a similar, but smaller, toy dog. Its name was Cocoa Junior because I wanted to be just like my brother.

We played hard with our toys, and Cocoa Junior developed holes or rips on several occasions. Each time I cried, worrying the stuffing would come out, and I would be left only with bits of his outside plush. My mother would tell me not to worry, because Mrs. Bosch would be coming soon and would fix him. She did, and her handiwork was better than that of any surgeon I have met, as she never left any trace of Cocoa Junior's wounds when she was through.

When my brother and I were not making demands on her, my mother spent all her spare time studying in those years. In the two years following, when she wrote her dissertation, she sat at our polished wood dining room table where she could also watch the two of us as we played in the living room. Eventually, she typed the completed dissertation on the manual typewriter my father bought her, but she did the initial draft, and many revisions, in pen on lined yellow paper. Years later, we still had that same dining room table, and bits of her work could still be seen, etched in the wood surface.

Her degree, I now understand, was at least as hard-won as

my M.D. She never had the privilege of worrying about only her own needs, as I did, while she worked toward her doctorate. As an adult, I learned that she paid the tuition for her master's degree at the University of Michigan by delivering phone books and catalogs when she was a young woman. Her parents, who had considerable means, had paid her college tuition, but hadn't approved of her decision to attend graduate school. They'd wanted her to marry and settle down right after college. Her two brothers were encouraged to go to professional school, and their parents paid for their studies.

By the time she married my father, at twenty-eight, my mother was considered an "old maid," and at thirty, when she had her first child, she was considered an "elderly mother." The tuition for her doctorate was paid for by a combination of my father's salary and loans from Rutgers.

In contrast, my parents paid every penny of my medical school tuition. I, too, married at twenty-eight; by the 1980s, this was considered "just the right time" for a professional woman to marry. I had Max right before my thirtieth birthday, and it was considered perfect timing for a first child.

The doctors thirty years earlier had thought Max's hypoxic episode may have some relationship to SIDS, and other babies in the family have had unusual breathing patterns as newborns. Andrew's death had not, of course, been my fault.

Still, the timing of the dream was uncanny. I wished I had an explanation. So many things in my life defied explanation. Back then I still believed that the world and my own experiences should make sense. I hadn't yet learned that life is full of questions that have no answers.

The second dream is a recurrent one. You have returned to the living world. I don't know how I know this, but I know you are back, as though back from a long trip abroad before cellphones and emails made communication across the world possible. You look the same in this dream as you always did to me—sturdy, your hair a mass of dark brown curls that, even after sixty, even after death, only have a few random silver strands. But your face is deeply lined with stress and worry. I know you look like this, but in the dream, I am not with you. I long to see you. I have so much to say, so much to tell you, so much to ask. I want to know what happened, where you have been, why you left.

It is all I want, all I have seemed to want forever, in this dream, but you refuse me. I try to call, frantically try to reach you, and you don't answer. You are out there, but I can't find you, and you have somehow let me know you will see my brother, you will be with other people, but you don't want to see me. You want nothing to do with me.

I have had this dream many times. Sleep experts, psychiatrists, and scientists now write that dreams in themselves mean nothing. If we interpret them, we are making up a meaning. Dreams, these experts say, are just leftover mental "junk" from our days. Detritus.

If that is true, why do we dream recurrently? Why is the dream of arriving for a test, having forgotten to study or unable to find the right room, a dream that is common to people who have gone to school? Why are dreams of being chased, or of falling, seemingly ubiquitous?

I can't dismiss the dream about my mother. She rejects me, abandons me again and again and again in my dreamscape. I awake from it exhausted, grieving, anguished. It takes hours for my psyche to adjust to the idea that it didn't actually happen.

My father was never able to clear my mother's things out of the house after she died. A year later, I went through her clothes and jewelry, her books and assorted odds and ends. My father told me to take anything I wanted. I thought I wanted some of her things. I had coveted some of her jewelry and other accessories when she was alive. I took them, but only wore a few pieces, the ones that made me feel closer to her, like the earrings she'd worn to my wedding and an antique onyx and marcasite pin, in the shape of a woman swimming, that I had given to her for her birthday a few years earlier. (A swimmer because my mother loved swimming. It was always her form of exercise. As far as I knew, she was still swimming two or three times a week at the Y in the months before she'd died.) The rest I kept in a drawer, realizing I'd never really wanted them; I just liked how they'd looked on her.

I gave away her books. I had already read many of them in her study. When I was an older child and teen, she saw psychotherapy clients in an office attached to our home. She had a rosewood desk in the office along with a matching chair with a black, cushioned seat, two blue-and-white patterned easy chairs, and a pale blue leather sofa. On three walls were soft, inoffensive framed prints. The fourth wall was entirely lined with rosewood bookshelves filled with textbooks and shorter works by famous psychologists and psychiatrists, including Anna Freud, Hilde Bruch, and Carl Rogers.

I would sometimes sneak in and read her psychology books when she wasn't there. I wanted to know what she knew, what she did in her office with those other people, many of them children, while her own children were just a few steps away in the kitchen or den. I was fascinated with the chapters on psychopathology, especially personality disorders and addictions. When one of my friends in high school stopped eating, lost weight, and threw away the lunches and snacks her mother packed for her, I had already read books about anorexia nervosa published in the early 1980s after Karen Carpenter died of the disease. I told my mother what my friend was doing but didn't tell her that I'd made a diagnosis. She alerted my friend's mother, as I knew she would.

I don't know whether my mother knew I was reading her textbooks when I was young.

I'm not even sure why I kept it a secret; perhaps I thought she would forbid it, saying the information was inappropriate for someone my age. Looking back now, though, I doubt it. Intellectual curiosity was encouraged in my home, and nobody stopped me from reading the novels and poetry in our den from the time I was quite young. I remember reading Joyce Carol Oates and Doris Lessing when I was eleven or twelve (not that I really understood them), and these novels were surely more controversial than psychology books. More likely, I felt like I shouldn't be treading on my mother's sacred professional ground. She didn't talk about her work with her clients, and I might have believed that it was the whole of psychology, not just the client information, that was a deep, dark secret.

Rosalind Kaplan

In some ways, psychology was a deep, dark secret in our family. I would not find out until much later that both my parents suffered with depression at various times in their lives, that people in both their families had been hospitalized for psychiatric problems, and one of my father's aunts had died by suicide. I knew that my brother struggled socially and was sometimes hard to get along with, but he was also very, very smart and had skipped a grade in school. So, his attention deficit hyperactivity disorder was not diagnosed until we were adults. These issues always lurked under the surface of my "normal," two-parent, suburban, upper-middle-class life, like a shark circling, waiting to surface and attack. Still, I knew nothing consciously until I was a teen.

My own depression and anxiety didn't officially present until I was an adult, but I now know that as a child, I was unusually anxious. Nobody ever told me it wasn't "normal" to worry constantly, to be afraid to be away from my family overnight, to need the light on in the hallway, the door to my room open in order to fall asleep, to obsess about being "bad" when in fourth grade I accidentally damaged a school textbook by getting crayon marks in it.

That my own mother was doing psychotherapy with other children and adults but didn't question her own daughter's discomfort living in the world is a sad irony. I think now that it spoke to both denial and distraction on her part. The denial seems self-explanatory. The distraction, I believe, came from many places: her own family of origin, who had not been warm to her or accepted her for who she was; her work, with which she was often preoccupied; my brother, whose issues caused obvious problems in functioning (as opposed to mine, which were internal, and could easily be masked by avoiding the situations that provoked anxiety).

Surely, my father's long work hours and frequent travel as an executive at a scientific publishing company, which frequently left my mother to manage the house, the children, and her career on her own, left her overwhelmed much of the time.

As a young child, I craved time and attention from my mother. I didn't pursue it the way some children did, by being a squeaky wheel. Instead, I tried to be good, to not make trouble, and hoped I would be rewarded by having my needs noticed.

My mother would come into my room to kiss me goodnight, and I always wanted her to stay, sitting on my bed, talking to me, for longer than she did, but she always seemed to have something more important to do.

In elementary school we went home from school for lunch and returned afterward. I was a latch-key child. I wished she would be home at lunchtime like the other mothers instead of leaving my lunch for me in the refrigerator to be eaten in front of the television, and that she, instead of an after-school babysitter, would be there after school.

Soon I gave up and retreated to television, books, and playing outside in our cul-de-sac with the neighborhood kids. I begged for a dog, which I never got, but pretended my gerbils and guppies were "real" pets. I took music lessons and practiced piano and flute, hoping that, with time, I could develop the musical talent my brother had, but it just wasn't there. I tried visual art classes but was pretty average at that, too.

Finally, in high school, I settled for being a straight-A student, which made my father proud, a reasonably good ballet and jazz dancer, and a social butterfly. It didn't make my mother pay more attention to me, but by high school, having a less attentive mother had its perks. She periodically complained about driving me to dance rehearsals and friends' houses when she wasn't working, and about my narcissistic interest in my clothes and appearance, but at least she didn't have to worry about something being wrong with me. Once I could drive, I pretty much fended for myself.

Maybe it was my childhood wish for more attention that had triggered my recurrent dream of her rejection. Or maybe it was my fantasy that, if she knew what my life was like without her, she would be angry. I had taken her possessions. I had always taken from her, part of me said. And I was getting everything in life she had wanted, but couldn't quite have.

I got a big career. I didn't just go to medical school, I went to an Ivy League medical school, and I didn't just work, I got recognition for my work. I got promoted, had some research publications, and achieved low-level notoriety as the doctor who all the women on the Main Line of Philadelphia wanted to see.

I got a husband who shared the housework and childcare and didn't leave me to diaper babies while he moved up the ranks and traveled to foreign countries for his work.

And I got to be a writer, to publish a book and some essays and even went to a writers' group and to writers' conferences.

My mother had wanted to be a writer. She wrote poems and, in her forties, a novel based on the psychology clinic where she worked—and where she couldn't get promoted or manage the interesting cases because she was a woman. Her writing, though, never really got off the ground. The novel sat in a drawer to be rediscovered after she died when my father moved out of the house and we cleared the last of her papers away.

Even with all this, I still got my two kids, a boy and a girl, just like she'd had.

And finally, maybe most importantly, I haven't had a difficult mother to struggle with my entire adult life.

By contrast, my maternal grandmother, Helen, was a force to be reckoned with. My mother's stories of her childhood were tales of emotional deprivation and cruelty: her mother telling her she was not pretty enough to have more than two dresses to wear to school, checking her ears and fingernails for dirt in front of her friends, giving away my mother's dog while she was at school one day because it had urinated in the house. She didn't tell me any of this until I was an adult. She had needed me to love my grandmother so my grandmother could love me.

My own experience of Helen when I was a child was ambivalent. My grandparents spoiled me in the typical way, buying me toys and clothes and letting me have ice cream every night during a visit to their home in Ohio, but I somehow knew it was all predicated on my being "good." I was a quiet and orderly child most of the time, but if I stepped out of line, roughhousing with my brother or had a tantrum when I was over-tired, the disapproval was palpable. The air would immediately take on a chill. I was always a little afraid when I was with my grandmother.

Throughout my childhood and adolescence, my mother talked to her parents on the phone at least once a week, except for when there was a falling out. Periodically, maybe once or twice a year, my mother and grandmother would have an explosive fight, either at the end of a visit or over the phone. Then they would stop speaking, and my mother would cry every day. I either never knew or have conveniently forgotten what those fights were about.

Eventually, my mother would become exhausted and give in, though she never felt she should. My grandmother's will was as strong as a diamond and as sharp as a razor blade.

Resolution and the return to normalcy required repeated apologies from my mother, flowers sent to Ohio, acquiescence to whatever terms Helen dictated. While I wasn't there to witness it, my father told me the pattern continued after I left home, and my mother was arguing with her parents only a couple of days before she died.

As a teenager, I wondered why my mother was always the one to fold. Why didn't she just tell Helen to take a hike? My mother was a professional woman with a home and a family and money of her own. Why would she let someone hurt her like that, make her cry, and then make her beg and plead for forgiveness for something she hadn't done?

If I have learned nothing else from losing my mother at a young age, I have learned this: she let it happen because she needed her mother.

Had my mother lived longer, I don't think we would have had the tumultuous, toxic, and painful relationship with each other that she and Helen had. We often had good times together and friendly phone calls. Nevertheless, it was not an easy relationship. Because I felt she'd often been emotionally absent when I was young, I sometimes blamed that, blamed her, for the anxiety and depression I battled off and on as a young adult. I also felt she resented me at times.

She confirmed this for me by saying, when we did clash, that I was selfish and entitled. In my teens and twenties, I knew definitively that those were two of the worst traits a person—no, a *woman*—could have.

STILL HEALING

What would my life be like if you were still here? Would I have fought and struggled with you? Would I have felt smothered by you or beholden to you? Would I resent caring for you in old age, as many of my friends now resent their parents at the end of their long lives?

Maybe so. But I also would have had your company, your support when you had it to give, the wisdom you had and imparted in tiny aliquots through my life. Remember when I was ten and I worried a lot? You told me to set aside half an hour a day for worrying, and then worry hard during that time, but not any other time. You know, it works! I've even suggested trying it to some of my own patients. They say it helped them.

If you had stuck around, my children would have had you as a grandmother who loved them with sheer abandonment, the way you loved Max for those few months. That would have been good for them.

I did okay with my kids, but I could have used your help. I didn't know what I was doing, and I had to make it all up as I went along. Max is brilliant, by the way. It's hard raising a kid who's too smart for his own good. Maddy is unusually sensitive. Maybe like you. Like me. That was hard, too. I hope I gave them what they needed to thrive.

I could have used a parent when I was depressed, when I was sick, when I was unsure. I know you couldn't give me as much as I wanted, but I would have taken whatever you were able to give.

You left me too soon. I still needed you. I ended up okay, but I still needed you.

My daughter, Maddy, now in her twenties, brought me a gift the last time she visited: a delicate silver chain with a rose gold charm. The charm is in the shape of a hat with cat ears, a representation of the pink "pussy hat" that many of the participants in the 2017 Women's March on Washington, D.C. wore. I was in D.C. that day, wearing my hand-knitted bright pink hat, the ears a bit asymmetrical, demonstrating my less-than-optimal knitting skills. Maddy knew how proud I was to be part of that march, so when she saw this necklace in a shop, she decided to buy it for me, especially when she found out part of the proceeds from its sale benefited a charity that assists victims of sexual violence.

When I opened the box it came in, a memory from more than twenty years ago drifted over me.

March 1986. I was in medical school in Philadelphia. The March for Women's Lives, a rally for reproductive rights to be held in Washington, D.C., was coming up and was expected to be massive. I planned to go and mentioned this to my mother. She was fifty-eight at the time, the same age I am as I write this. She asked, "May I go with you?"

I was surprised, as she never liked big crowds. I fretted a bit about how she'd cope, especially if the weather turned bad. I warned her about the long bus ride we would have to take, the paucity of clean bathrooms, the need to bring our own food and water, the long day and sore feet we would likely have, but she still wanted to go.

I needn't have worried. My mother was right in her element, holding up a sign saying "Mothers for Choice," chanting, marching, sitting on the grass on the Mall and cheering during speeches given by N.O.W. leadership.

How could I have forgotten? This was who my mother was. She was someone who cared about issues, about women, about equality and fairness. Someone who had given part of her life to improving the lives of others through her work, someone who had done the best she could to raise two children to be moral people, and someone who put together the best life she could for herself despite the obstacles her family and the times and society put in front of her.

I had another dream about you that night, after Maddy gave me the necklace. You look like you did before you died, not old or frail, but I know, in the dream, you are older. I am in your house in New Jersey with you. In the dream, I am myself, the age I am now. The house has too much furniture in it. So much furniture in some of the rooms that it is hard to walk around it. The furniture includes what you had in your house, but also some of the furniture from my house, and some from your mother's house.

I tell you I want to move the furniture around so it fits better, and that maybe we don't need all of it. I think you are going to protest, to tell me it is your house, and you don't want me changing it. But you don't. You say, "Go ahead. You can do what you think is best." You sit there, watching, while I rearrange things. When I'm done, you agree that the new way is better.

Perhaps dreams don't really mean anything in themselves. Maybe some of us just interpret this "junk," this mental detritus, to make meaning out of the detritus of our lives. For me it doesn't matter; over time my dreams have helped me make peace with losing my mother in such a strange, seemingly meaningless way—a way that afforded no opportunity for any resolution between us. They have allowed me to see my mother in all her complexity. To appreciate what was good and forgive the rest.

I still think you left me too soon. I still needed you. You hadn't completed your work. You weren't done with what you were doing, not just for me, but also for yourself. But you paved the way for me to do my work. My path had fewer obstacles than yours. You made sure of that, and I guess that's going to have to be enough.

EIGHT

Some Matters of Choice

Summer of 1982

I lead a young woman across Commonwealth Avenue in Boston, my left arm wrapped around her shoulders. I pretend I don't hear the shouts and jeers around us, pretend we are just crossing the street, not plowing through a crowd of protesters on the median strip. I behave as though I don't hear the footsteps behind us, following us to the sidewalk in front of the clinic, an unassuming brownstone in a row of nearly identical brownstones, most of which were once large homes but have been converted to apartment buildings or offices.

Saturdays at New England Women's Service are marked by large groups of protestors armed with oaktag signs saying *Jesus died for your sins* and *The heart is beating at 6 weeks,* and with jars with what appear to be intact human fetuses in them, though they could be some other species, like the fetal pigs we dissected during AP Biology in high school. Or maybe they are just blobs of flesh-colored plastic floating in water. The protesters yell, "Baby killers!" and "Murderers" and "Don't do it! Let us save your baby!" They thrust the jarred fetuses into the sightline of anyone attempting to pass them. We, the staff, must escort those women who arrive alone to the clinic past this disturbing display.

My client, a petite brunette named Susan and wearing denim shorts and a T-shirt, is shaking as we approach the throng. I feel a hot tear fall on my arm. Despite the clinic's briefing on what they will face on a Saturday morning, clients are never ready for the reality of these people and the aggressive certitude of their version of good and evil.

I've learned to slam through, forge ahead, and help my clients process this assault after we are safely inside. It's best to be quick and ruthless on the way in.

By the time we reach the bland, generic waiting room with its rows of vinyl-upholstered chairs and beige Formica reception counter encased in Plexiglass, Susan has regained some equilibrium. She breathes in the scent of antiseptic and fear that permeates this space, registers the tearful teenager glaring at her mother in the corner, and the stoic couple slumped, dry-eyed and stony-faced, by the window.

"Is it like that every day?" she asks me as I lead her toward a chair. "I didn't think they'd get that close to us. I definitely didn't think they'd touch us!"

"It's the worst on weekends," I reply. "On the weekdays, a lot of folks are working, so it's only the most vocal of them, the diehards. I know it feels overwhelming, but nobody has gotten violent, at least." I couldn't know that a dozen years later, two similar women's clinics in Brookline, a suburb only minutes away, would be the target of a shooting rampage by an antiabortion protester. In that attack, two staffers would be killed and five others wounded.

I hand her a clipboard with medical history and consent forms. "Here. You need to fill these out. You have about a half an hour before we'll call you back. Is there anything you need? Any questions I can answer right now? You'll have time to talk with me just before your procedure. I'll check that you're sure this is what you want, and we'll go over these forms."

I first met Susan ten days ago, at her intake. She was about eight weeks pregnant then, single, twenty-three-years-old. The father was married and lived in Atlanta. He'd given her the money for a termination but didn't want to father her child. Her parents, strict Catholics, would likely have disowned her if they learned of the pregnancy and certainly would shun her if they found out she'd had an abortion. Damned if you do, damned if you don't.

During that first session, she wasn't sure about the decision to terminate. She grappled with her own needs, her guilt and her fears. She didn't feel that abortion was a sin or that it was murder; she just wasn't sure if it was the right choice for her. She reviewed her options: parenthood, adoption, abortion. She finally concluded that the latter was the only one she could reasonably choose right now. Her ambivalence was typical, contrary to the belief by some that women take the decision to abort lightly. I don't think I ever counseled a client who didn't struggle.

As her counselor, part of my job with Susan is to provide information on the termination procedure as well as resources if she chooses to carry her pregnancy to term. More importantly, I must listen and reflect her own words back to her to assist her in making a decision. My opinion is irrelevant; I will not offer my own thoughts.

I had little formal training for this, save my college psychology courses. I also had little in the way of life experience, having just completed my undergraduate education. I learned what to do by listening to the other lay counselors work with their clients. I took the job at New England Women's Service at the bidding of a friend who worked there and thought I'd be a good fit. I worked Wednesday evenings and Saturday mornings.

On the weekdays, I had a job in a lab at Dana-Farber Cancer Research Center, extracting DNA from human endothelial cells for a post-doctoral biochemistry fellow who was hoping to clone a human clotting factor to treat hemophilia. Though the DNA extractions were successful, we had so far failed miserably at producing the agent. My work there was repetitive, solitary, and soul-sucking, such that I was reconsidering my plan to apply for a PhD in biochemistry. Even if the clotting factor project took off, a clinical product was far in the future. It would be years before patients would benefit. But at New England Women's Service, I'd been given a chance to make a direct difference, one client at a time. I also believed in the mission—a safe space for women's reproductive and sexual health—and hoped we might help shape a feminist future.

Fall, 1982

Once I'd made the decision to apply to medical school instead of applying for a PhD, things moved quickly. I had completed the prerequisite courses during college and taken the Medical College Admission Test the previous summer, "just in case." In the late summer of '82, I wrote my "personal statements" and filled in med school applications.

My husband and I joke that we would never get into medical school now with the credentials we'd had back in the '80s. Medical applicants today are not just A students and good test-takers. They have polish and poise and, often, talents and life experience I couldn't even imagine at that time in my life. But at the time, I was considered a strong candidate and granted multiple interviews, including my top two choices: University of Pennsylvania School of Medicine and Columbia College of Physicians and Surgeons.

The interview at University of Pennsylvania was pleasantly unmemorable. I liked my brief introduction to Philadelphia, and I felt comfortable with the third-year medical student who showed me around and housed me overnight. My interview day at Columbia was a very different story.

I arrived in Manhattan from Boston by train, clad in a navy-blue skirt suit and a striped, ruffle-collared blouse, the "uniform" of female med school applicants at the time. It was a far cry from the hippie dresses I wore in the women's clinic or the jeans and T-shirts we all sported under our lab coats at Dana-Farber. Emerging from the subway at 168th Street, I noted a heavy police presence, complete with German shepherd K-9 officers. The Washington Heights neighborhood of Manhattan was plagued by violence related to crack cocaine in those days, an issue I'd not encountered in Boston and had failed to consider before applying to Columbia. Now I wondered if I'd feel safe here. Would I want to make this part of Manhattan my home for four years?

I forgot about the police dogs when I reached the heavy wood door of the College of Physicians and Surgeons administrative building. Inside I navigated a long, empty hallway tiled in black and white marble, silent but for the clicking of the heels of my navy pumps as I approached the admissions office. After checking in with a receptionist, I was seated in an alcove along with another prospective student, a nervous young man also dressed in navy, to wait for my interview.

Half an hour later, and long after the young man had been led away by a faculty member, a tall, silver-haired man in a long, white coat rushed toward the alcove. By this time I'd become increasingly anxious, wondering if they'd forgotten about me or if, perhaps, the offer of an interview had been a mistake they had now discovered.

"Rosalind?" he asked.

"Yes." I leapt up from my seat a little too quickly and without grace.

"I'm Dr. X. I'm sorry for the delay," he told me. "I was just asked to interview you a few minutes ago. The faculty member who was assigned to your interview noted, on examining your file this morning, that he knows your father quite well, so he recused himself."

I froze for a second. Yes, my father, the CEO of a scientific publishing company, knew lots of academic researchers. Of course, it was ethical to recuse oneself if a preexisting relationship would render one biased. But it was not my father he was interviewing—it was me, and I was a separate person, an adult with my own strengths and weaknesses. Perhaps the original interviewer was afraid that if he contributed to my rejection, my father would throw his next manuscript in the slush pile. Still, this set me at a disadvantage, being interviewed by someone who might resent the sudden intrusion on his time and who'd had only a few minutes to review my application.

"Yes, I understand. My dad knows lots of medical researchers. Thank you for doing this on short notice." I had no idea that I'd soon feel anything but thankful.

Dr. X led me to a small conference room where we sat at a round, dark wood table. He laid my open file in front of him and cleared his throat.

"I'll get right to the important questions. Your qualifications, like those of our other interviewees, are impressive, so I'd like to ask you about your way of thinking. I noticed in your employment history that you're working at a women's health clinic," he stated.

"Yes, New England Women's Service. I've been working there part-time since I graduated from Brandeis."

"Is the facility an abortion provider?" he asked.

"Yes, we do provide terminations, among other services, like contraception, Pap smears, and STD (sexually transmitted disease) testing."

His face remained calm, impassive, as he paused. He seemed to be thinking for a minute. "So," he slowly began, "if you were confronted with a person, say a friend or a colleague, who told you she was planning to kill herself, would you attempt to stop her?"

"Well, yes, of course," I replied. I was surprised, even confused, by his line of questioning. The answer seemed obvious. "I mean, assuming the person was not terminally ill and wanting to end her life because of intractable pain, I would certainly want to stop her and would take action to do so."

"Mmm." He gritted his teeth at me. They were white and even. His canine teeth looked unusually sharp. "Let's leave the idea of euthanasia for later. I find your answer highly inconsistent with your work in the clinic."

"How so?" I asked. I needed to know where he was headed with this. My *modus operandi* in previous interviews had screamed "good girl" and "pleaser," but I felt a different voice rising up in my chest in this room.

He sighed and began speaking in what seemed like a falsely patient, patronizing tone. "Well, one either takes the view that preservation of life is foremost, so that preventing suicide and preventing abortion are both appropriate. Or one takes the libertarian view in which people can do what they wish. They can kill themselves or abort their child."

"I disagree!" I blurted, aghast. I had never thought of my mindset as "inconsistent." I also was pretty sure he shouldn't be asking me about views on a politically and religiously charged issue, but I no longer cared. I needed to speak my mind.

"Your contention," I continued, "only makes sense if you believe an embryo or a fetus before twelve weeks of gestation is a person, a life. Not everybody believes that."

"Ah, so you don't believe that a fetus is a life?"

I was in deep shit now. So much for admission to Columbia.

"No, I don't, not an independent life. The fetus can't exist at that point outside the mother's body. I won't say a fetus has no value, that it is not to be considered, but I believe the physical and emotional well-being of the mother takes precedence."

My interviewer stared at me. I don't know what he was thinking; I'll never know. I don't remember how the interview ended, nor do I remember leaving the building. The next thing I can recall is being on the street near the subway stop. I stared at the large, sharp teeth of a German shepherd who lay, panting, next to an officer stationed at the entrance to the C train. *Perhaps Washington Heights just isn't meant to be my home,* I thought.

A week went by. I was back in Boston, plating cell cultures and running gel chromatographs. I assumed my rejection letter from Columbia would soon arrive in the mail.

Instead, I arrived home one evening to find a message on my answering machine from the admissions office at the College of Physicians and Surgeons.

"Your interviewer recused himself from your application," said the female voice on the phone. "He said that the two of you had philosophical differences. We'd like you to return for another interview."

One version of this story, a version I have tried to tell myself through the years, is that Dr. X realized that our "philosophical differences" were not a reflection on my character, that he voluntarily bowed out of Columbia's decision on my application. I want to believe this. It would mean actual ethical thinking can prevail, that discourse between people of different beliefs and backgrounds is possible. Maybe humans can actually live and let live if this version were reality. Yet my experience in the years since then leads me to believe another scenario was much more likely: Dr. X was forced to recuse himself by the admissions committee when they learned he was asking politically charged questions. The committee would have feared legal action or at least a slap on the wrist. That abortion was the specific topic could even constitute gender discrimination, and no university wants to risk such an accusation. Offering me another interview, one that would go well, would have been damage control.

I returned to Washington Heights a few weeks later to meet with a different faculty member, a sixtyish woman with long, silver hair in a bun, wearing a hippie-style dress, who invited me into her lab for the interview.

"We need more smart women here," she told me. "And I like that you are helping women at the clinic in Boston."

I felt at home with her, and we talked easily. I suppose I should have felt a sense of relief, of redemption, when I left. Instead, I felt duped.

A few days later my acceptance letter to Columbia College of Physicians and Surgeons arrived in the mail. I tacked it on the bulletin board alongside my University of Pennsylvania acceptance, telling myself I'd make a decision before the deadline in the spring. That I would not jump to any conclusions. In my heart, though, the decision was already made. I could handle urban crime and dogs with sharp teeth, but I knew I'd never really feel safe there.

Spring, 1983

The women's dorm at the hostel in Amsterdam reminded me of the barracks in *Hogan's Heroes*: dark, a little dusty, metal bunk beds covered in threadbare sheets, and dark green, itchy wool blankets. Still, the mattresses were thick enough and neither sagging nor lumpy. Better yet, Dutch breakfast was included, and coffee was available all day in the dining room. The dorm accommodated twelve, and most of the bunks were laden with backpacks and books and clothing tossed aside when the occupants went out. Still, the day Karen and I arrived, there were only a few people roaming the building. We chose two empty bottom bunks, tossing our sweatshirts onto them and forcing our heavy packs underneath the bedframes.

The place was far from luxurious. It lacked the rustic, picturesque features of even the cheapest inns and hotels in which we'd stayed earlier in our backpacking tour of Europe.

Nevertheless, I thought it a good find. We were close to the end of our trip, and the hostel allowed us to stretch the little bit of money we had left. I had to admit that our orange paperback copy of *Let's Go Europe 1983* had served us well, leading us to lodging that was safe and reasonably clean. When you're twenty-two-years old and close to broke, you have to be willing to give up some of the icing if you want the cake. For us, the cake was two months traveling Western Europe, and we wanted it. It was a last taste of freedom for us before we began our professional training—I would be starting medical school in Philadelphia at the end of the summer, and Karen was pursuing a doctorate in psychology—and, presumably, our "real lives."

Surprisingly, the women's dorm became quite lively in the late evening, a kind of multinational slumber party. We compared travel notes with a couple of German women. Karen played cards with three university students from Sweden. Everyone swapped stories, took photos together, braided hair, and complained about the scratchy blankets. Everyone, that is, except one young woman, who stayed to herself on her bed in the corner of the room, her head in a paperback book.

I'd seen this woman, or maybe girl, alone in the hallway earlier. I greeted her in English, and she'd given me a little smile but didn't speak. Small and raven-haired, with big, dark eyes, she was strikingly pretty, even in the jeans and oversized hoodie she'd been wearing. *Maybe she doesn't speak English or, for that matter, doesn't share a language with any of the other travelers,* I thought, *or maybe she just wants to be left alone.* I probably would have let her be if I hadn't entered the communal bathroom that first evening and stumbled upon her sitting on the floor, head in hands.

"Are you okay?" I reflexively asked, forgetting she might not understand me.

She looked up, startled, and I could see she'd been crying. She nodded slowly. "Yes, I'm all right," she finally said.

"You speak English."

"Yes, a little."

I slid down the cinder block wall by the sink and sat on the dirty bathroom floor with her.

I don't know how it happened, but we found ourselves in conversation. It was the sort of connection that sometimes happens between two women, which I can only attribute to a primal sense of sisterhood, an instinctual recognition of oneself in another person.

Her name was Elena, and she was just nineteen-years-old, a university student in Madrid.

Her English was good, which was lucky, since I didn't know more than two or three words in Spanish. She'd come to Amsterdam alone, she told me. Her family, with whom she lived, had no idea she was there.

"If they knew, they would never want to speak to me again," she told me. S

he didn't need to say more; I already knew why she'd come.

"It's illegal in Spain, isn't it?" I asked.

She nodded. "I could be arrested for what I am doing, put in jail. It's against everything I was taught to believe. My religion, my family. Even my boyfriend. I don't know what he'd do if he found out. But I don't want to stay with him, and I can't have a child alone. I borrowed money from my friend; she made the appointment for me. My parents think I'm with this friend in Barcelona."

"So, you're going to a clinic by yourself? When?"

You can probably guess the rest. This is how Karen and I ended up going to an abortion clinic in Amsterdam with a girl we barely knew. We took the cab ride with Elena the next morning and sat in the cramped, musty waiting area while she had her procedure. We rode back to the hostel with her, tucked her into her bunk with two scratchy blankets, and made her tea in the dining room. Not just to be nice but because, but because, well, what if it was one of us, alone and scared in a strange city? Only that could never happen to us, to American women, right?

January 21, 2017

Karen and I, and half million other people, are wearing bright pink, hand-knit hats with pussy ears. We are walking up Pennsylvania Avenue in Washington, D.C., when we get separated, losing track of each other in the dense crowds. The Women's March, the largest single-day protest in American history, snakes through the streets. There are so many people here that cellphone towers are jumbled; there is no way we can find each other until we return to the chartered bus that brought us here and is now parked outside the city. *No matter,* I think. *I'll make the best of this.*

We're marching because Donald Trump has been inaugurated President of the United States. We know human rights, including a woman's right to choose whether or not to carry a pregnancy to term, are in peril. We're afraid, and it feels like there is not much we can do. So, we march and chant: "Racist, sexist, anti-gay, Donald Trump go away." We wear our pink pussy hats and carry signs that read, "Pussy Grabs Back."

We're afraid but not of the enormous crowd or the lack of phone service or being separated. This march is peaceful. In fact, there is not a single arrest, despite the massive numbers of protestors. Even separated from my friend, I don't feel alone here. Everyone around me is friendly, and we are all passionate about what we want, and what we want is tolerance and human decency, and the equality that we thought was coming decades ago but then never did.

What we fear is not what's here today, at this march, but what this next period of time will mean for women's futures. It's a good thing we didn't know exactly what would happen in the coming years. If we had, the fear might have paralyzed us, rendering hundreds of thousands of women inert in the streets of D.C.

I am walking along the route with strangers now, a group of women who have "adopted" me after Karen and I lost track of each other.

One of them, a woman about my age in a red jacket and jeans, says, "It's cool how many people have shown up. But I keep asking myself, *How can we be here? How are we fighting the same battles over and over and over? How did we take so many steps forward and so many more steps back?*"

I agree. "My mother fought these battles for herself and for me, and now I am fighting them again for myself and my daughter, and we are still 'less than.' We're still earning less, picking up the second shift, doing the dirty work, relegated to the margins. We're still bitches and cunts when we stand up for ourselves, and prey when we don't."

"Hell, yeah," says another woman, a younger woman with dark, curly hair. "Think about it. The leader of the free world 'grabs pussies' and nobody stops him."

I wonder where I've been for the last three decades. I'd stopped fighting sexism in the public realm as I struggled to raise my own children and do my job. I wasn't naïve; it wasn't complacency, or a belief the work was done, that stopped me from fighting for reproductive rights and against the glass ceiling. Part of it was disappointment in the wave of feminism I rode in my early adulthood; the reality of my life as a privileged, educated, white woman is that to do the work I was trained to do, I needed to lean on other, less privileged women to manage my home and care for my children. I began to understand intersectionality, to see where "second- wave feminism" had failed, but I had no idea what to do about it. Meanwhile, backlash against progress already made was mounting, and the risk of losing ground became reality.

Still, I've been fighting my personal battles as a woman in the world, as a mother, and as a female doctor. Especially as a doctor, a role in which I've seen, up close, the toll sexism, racism, and economic disparities take on health. *The personal is political*, the feminist movement declared in my youth. Yes, and the political is personal. I'm ready to be publicly vocal again. I'm happy we are here at this march, but angry we need to be here.

October 2021

Texas. My daughter lives in Texas. Okay, Austin, to be fair, the "blue city in the red state," but still, she is a young woman in Texas, where being a woman is becoming increasingly dangerous.

"Mom!" she says to me, trying to get me to shut up as I rant on the phone that she MUST MOVE OUT OF TEXAS RIGHT NOW!

"I'm okay here. I'm not going to need an abortion. You taught me to take better care of myself than that. I'm not in rural Texas; lots of people in Austin believe in reproductive freedom. I love my job here. I'm not ready to go anywhere right now."

Texas has just passed SB8, an ass-backward but legally crafty law that essentially has stopped abortion after six weeks of gestation in the state by allowing private parties to sue anyone performing or aiding and abetting an abortion after six weeks. It's the most restrictive law in this country since *Roe v. Wade* made the right to pregnancy termination a constitutional right.

Yes, true, my daughter is okay there. She has an education, a job, insurance, resources. If she ever needed an abortion, she could go to Oklahoma or Mexico, like so many women have had to do since SB8's advent. She'd do what Elena had in 1983, and nobody would have to know. But not everyone is so fortunate.

I try to tamp down my fury, but I am fired up. Texas has trumped every other state so far with a new normal in which the dangerous, illegal abortions of the pre-Roe era will be yet another way for Texan women to die. There is no ethical conversation, no "live and let live," no true discourse between those of disparate views. Now other states might follow suit. Maybe even other countries, carried by an anti-choice movement that keeps its finger on the pulse of the U.S. In 2021, ninety-five percent of women in Europe had access to "on-demand" abortion, at least within the first twelve weeks of pregnancy, but that, too, can change.

Even with FDA approval of medical abortion, otherwise known as the abortion pill or RU486, access to safe abortion is not guaranteed in the U.S. For one thing, a large swath of the women who may need RU486 don't even know it exists. Secondly, many state and local laws limit its use or ban it after six weeks' gestation. RU486 may safely be obtained through a telehealth visit from another state or another country, but in a place like Texas, a woman can be arrested for obtaining the medication illegally, and the state could go after providers who mail the medications to Texas residents. Obtaining it illegally on the Internet is an option, but then there is no screening for safety and no backup should it fail—another route to morbidity and death.

What happened to the days when the most distressing part of obtaining a first-trimester abortion was walking through a line of protestors waving fetal parts in jars in our faces?

Those days never went away; the backlash continued and then accelerated. Maybe a few decades ago, we thought Roe and the clinics of the '70s were an answer, but they were always just a few links in the delicate chain of gender equity, a chain that is incomplete and can so easily be broken, the parts disconnected, rendering women small and silent again. Access to abortion and birth control was never readily available for women without money, without care for already-born children, without insurance or time off from work to pursue care, without transportation and support systems. The less access, the more risk of spiraling further into joblessness and poverty, a never-ending cycle.

I imagine myself on the median strip of some godforsaken Texas road, a coffin with the body of a woman who has died in childbirth or from a botched self-induced abortion, a sign saying, "The adult heart continues to beat, and it can also break. Don't kill my sister, my daughter, my friend." Would that make them look? Would it make them see? I don't think so.

June 24, 2022

I'm drinking a latte in a library/café in Reykyavik, Iceland, where we're relaxing after a hiking trip in the southern part of the country. We will fly home to Philadelphia the next day. Out in nature all week, I've pushed COVID and politics and doctoring to the back of my mind, and I'm breathing more easily than usual. Until I look at my newsfeed, that is.

The Dobbs decision has come in from the Supreme Court just today, stating that the U.S. Constitution does not confer a right to abortion. *Roe v. Wade*, which has protected American women's right to choose whether to carry a fetus to term, has been overturned, and legislation regarding abortion has been returned to the states. Thirteen states already have abortion bans in place, and others are expected to follow suit.

I push my iPhone under Larry's nose, show him the headline, and then burst into tears.

I knew this was coming, but I've been holding out a tiny grain of hope. Larry tries to comfort me, but I feel inconsolable. The chain is broken, with little hope of repair now.

An Icelandic woman about my age, impeccably dressed, her graying blonde hair in a thick bun atop her head, approaches me and puts a hand on my shoulder.

"I'm so sorry for your country," she says softly, instinctively knowing what I've seen, why I'm crying. "This would never happen here, I think."

"Thank you," I reply. "Yes, I'm so sorry, too."

NINE

To A Patient

Dear Patient:
Your email says the pain is even worse, more than you can tolerate. You want me to give you instructions on what next to do. But here's the thing. I have run out of ideas. I have no plans. No new potions or lotions or patches or pills. No magic. I am without my wand. I have come to the end of my repertoire, and you know this but ask me anyway. I know this, but still rack my brain hoping for an answer to fly out of some forgotten crevice.

You have been everywhere, to everyone, to pain management doctors and neurologists and psychiatrists and rheumatologists and famous clinics where they poked and prodded you and maybe believed you or maybe didn't, and hypothesized and experimented, then sent you back.

You landed back at my door with nothing different, nothing new or better, after the failed epidurals and useless nerve stimulators, the trials of anesthetics and analgesics and anti- inflammatories and antidepressants, the muscle relaxants and anti-epileptics and neuroleptics and opioids and antagonists to opioids and cannabinoids and alpha blockers and beta blockers, and blockers of blocking...

So, I give you a new anti-inflammatory. I don't think it will work. It would take a miracle, but I'm all out of those, along with a lot of the hope I used to carry around in my black bag, where now there is just a stethoscope and some other instruments.

I don't know what being a doctor is anymore. What am I if the recipe is part drug dealer, part data entry clerk, part someone who argues with insurance company representatives who deny tests and medicines to my patients, plus a pinch of maternal comfort and a sprinkling of reassurance, a teaspoon of bad news, a drop of warning, a dash of advice, and as much hand- holding as I've got available? I used to diagnose, treat, and impart information to patients and students. Now, I compile metrics and choose codes for chart documentation and dispel myths that come from Internet chat rooms. I listen to the pain that comes from living shattered lives in a shattered world. I have no cure for that. Sometimes I can help someone feel less alone.

Sometimes someone yells at me because they are frustrated, and I let them. After they leave, I cry because I, too, am frustrated.

I go to a writing retreat. I go to write and let the words that clutter my mind leak out, float into the air: coronary dissection, dissecting aorta, aortic sclerosis, sclerosing cholangitis, cholangiocarcinoma, carcinoid syndrome, syndrome X, X-linked dominant, dominant personality, personality disorder, disordered eating...

How much is too much? High blood pressure, high cholesterol, high demands. How much is too little? Low heart rate, low blood count, low self-esteem. What is enough? Are thirty years long enough to try to help others? Long enough to put myself last? Is it enough that I've begun to feel your pain? Is it enough that I want, desperately, to help you, even though I don't have the tools and sometimes have no energy?

I know so much but not enough. Is less than everything nothing? Is less than everything failure? Do I need to start over? You know I can't start over even if I want to. I want to empty my mind, but the words won't leave. If I stop for a while, my stethoscope will cool, and the words will stop swirling and gusting and will settle into the sulci of my brain. I try to push you to the back of my mind, but it is not where you reside inside me.

Last week, I went to a writing retreat, to write and do yoga and rest. I dream, and in my dreams the lotions and potions and patches and pills emerge, and you ask me for help. Then one night, you appear, well and whole, and I wish I could have made that happen.

I woke with Maimonides' prayer on my lips: "In the sufferer let me see only the human being."

Forget the potions and pills, the specialists, the magic wand. Forget the metrics, the codes, the prior authorization. Go back to the beginning. Let me see you and hear you and stand with you in the Kingdom of the Sick for long enough that you know you are seen and heard and not alone. Let me use my pen to write you so others see who you are and what you bear.

This is the part of the recipe I had forgotten: I can't cure you. I can't take away your pain.

My job is not to make you whole, but to be as whole as I can be; to heal you with my own wholeness.

With love and respect,
Your Doctor

TEN

Shedding My Coat
Part I
No More White Coat

The day I walked away from my medical career, I'd been discouraged and sad and tired for so long I seemed to have no feelings left. I focused on the plan I'd made for the next year and tried not to think about what I was leaving.

I didn't depart suddenly. I didn't walk out in a huff or commit a dramatic act like throwing my computer monitor out the window, something I'd heard one frustrated doctor had done. The leaving was slow and labored and wracked with pain, like the last mile of an injured runner's marathon. I'd resisted even the thought of leaving for over a year. Then I entertained the idea for a year. Finally, I gave six months' notice in January of 2018, with a plan to stick it out until that June, the end of the medical academic year. I would complete the classes I taught that year, and transition as many of my patients as possible to new doctors in that time.

I'd cried at least half of the days over the preceding two years, overwhelmed by useless, administrative tasks that seemed to increase each week, lonely in an office full of doctors and staff with whom I was a poor fit, and mourning for what practicing medicine had once been but no longer was. When I wasn't crying, I was actively summoning the energy I needed to do my work. Each day during the last months of my position as an associate professor of medicine and a primary care doctor, I made sure to greet my patients with a smile. I tried to focus my attention on them rather than my computer monitor. I reminded myself to mentor my students, residents, and nurse practitioner with a firm but gentle hand. I wanted to leave with dignity, knowing I'd done the best I could.

I knew leaving my practice would be an end to a piece of myself, an end I had not expected to come to so soon. I had not lost my love of medicine, my patients, or teaching. What I'd lost was the ability to keep on going when a million obstacles studded the road each day— insurance mandates for prior authorization of medications and pre-certifications for tests that caused delays in care and hours of extra work each week. Ever-increasing demands for data collection and data entry. Multiple transitions from one electronic medical record to another. An office perpetually understaffed with undertrained employees. A patient panel so large that sick patients and patients needing follow-up care were unable to get appointments to see me. I'd let so much roll off me that my will to continue my work had simply eroded the way a cliff erodes when water runs down its face for years.

That last day, I completed as many of the tasks in my digital inbox as I could, and then forwarded the inbox to a colleague. I cleared the last papers and books from my desk. I emailed my student evaluations to the deans' office. I put my office key and ID badge on the office manager's desk.

Walking out the office door at the end of that day felt like walking through a portal in a science fiction story. On one side of the portal was everything I thought I knew about myself, my life, the world. On the other was . . .

Without my inbox, with no patient panel, no trainees, and no meetings to attend, I was superfluous to the medical community. Without my white coat and my ID badge, without a place I was supposed to show up the next morning, I felt invisible. Without my title and my tasks and obligations, I was nobody. Nothing. A puff of air. I might be transported on the wind to another time and place, blown like smoke curling up into the atmosphere and disappearing. If nobody needed me, what justified my existence?

Thirty years before, when I was finishing medical school, I never imagined practicing medicine could make me miserable. My four years in medical school at the University of Pennsylvania shimmer with a nostalgia that I now think must be constructed of distorted memories. I remember being happy.

One of the aspects I loved about med school was constant camaraderie. During the pre- clinical blocks that made up the first year and a half of my medical education, I spent half of most days in a lecture hall with the other ninety-nine students in my class. At first glance, we could have been any group of relatively clean-cut young adults. Some of the group sat, seemingly rapt, in the first few rows, writing as many of the professors' words as they could get down in their notebooks. Some were more *laissez-faire*, seated in the middle of the auditorium, legs crossed. A group of us knit during many of the lectures, knowing it was best to just listen, and then obtain the transcribed notes from the student assigned that day to note-service duty. The bolder, more disinterested or perhaps rebellious students, all men in my recollection, sat in the far back seats and read newspapers, folded and held below the level visible to the professors. They depended on notes and textbooks alone but knew absence from lectures was considered unacceptable.

When we weren't in lecture, we spent our time on lab activities—dissecting our cadavers in pairs in gross anatomy, working in groups of four as we examined slides of cells in pathology, or conducting experiments with electrolytes in physiology lab, or in study groups, reviewing material and quizzing each other.

On clinical rotations, I was part of a team of students, residents, and attendings in the hospital. We rounded on patients morning and evening, the attending doctor followed by the residents, all in their long, crisp white coats, students trailing behind in our short ones. Medical students could spend extra time talking with the patients after rounds and routine chores were complete for the day.

I still remember my very first patient on my Internal Medicine rotation, a grandmother of ten with silver curls and crinkly, laughing eyes, who invited me to sit with her when I entered her room to check on her vital signs. She knew I was a brand-new medical student. She told me the story of her recent lung disease, but by the end of our time together, she also asked me all the questions she still hadn't asked the doctors, hesitant to slow them down on rounds. While I couldn't answer many of them myself, I went back to the team and got the information she needed. The next day on rounds, she beamed at me and thanked me in front of the whole team.

I actually enjoyed studying when I wasn't in class, the lab, or the hospital, and I didn't really mind exams, even the National Board of Medical Examiners tests mandated periodically throughout medical school. I was also learning how to do clinical tasks—examining patients, drawing blood, interpreting lab studies, performing bedside procedures—and this was what I lived for. During a rotation at the Philadelphia V.A. Hospital, I was in charge of drawing blood and checking lab results for every patient on the team each day, then formulating an interpretation and tentative plan for abnormal lab values. By the end of the month, I felt proficient at these skills.

There were certainly aspects of medical school I didn't like. In the first-year gross anatomy lab, the sweet, cloying odor of the formaldehyde seemed to seep into my skin. For the entire first semester, I smelled it even after I changed out of the old, worn clothes I had dedicated to anatomy dissections, after showering, and even in my bed at night. I was never sure when it was real and when my brain's olfactory centers were conjuring the smell from memory.

Another part of medical school I found unappealing was my very first clinical rotation, General Surgery. I drew a bad number in the lottery that determined which students got first choice of the available locations that month. I ended up on a team dedicated to the early iterations of bariatric (weight-loss) surgery. Each day, we performed two or three stomach- stapling procedures on morbidly obese patients, with the goal of decreasing the amount of food they were able to ingest after surgery.

There were two medical students on the service each month, and our job in the operating room was to retract the abdominal fat of the patients on either side of the huge vertical incision so the surgeon could see inside the abdominal cavity. Each stomach-stapling took about two hours. The other medical student on my team, Harold, and I stood across from each other at the operating table, holding metal retractors clamped onto adipose tissue. The glistening yellow fat, attached to the overlying skin, was slippery, so there was a fine balance between the considerable traction required to hold back half of an abdominal wall and the hand pressure needed to keep the fat clamped into the retractor. It was exhausting, thankless work from which Harold and I learned essentially nothing, as we could not get close enough to the table to see any surgical technique. After retracting fat for two hours, my arm muscles burned from the exertion, so I was perpetually anxious for surgery to end. To top it off, the attending surgeon had a bad temper.

Any slip-ups by his residents, students, nurses, or staff would result in yelling, cursing, and sometimes the throwing of surgical instruments.

Yes, it was an abusive month. I didn't take it personally. I quietly made the decision that surgery was not for me. I did what was asked, read the portions of the surgery textbook assigned, and waited for a better rotation. Or maybe I don't remember it right. Maybe I was miserable.

Maybe I cried that month and wondered why I'd gone to med school. But if I did, that's not how I remember it. I saw it, like anatomy lab, as a means to an end.

Later rotations left much more positive impressions. By fourth year, I was doing sub-internships in medicine and psychiatry, rotations in which students acted as first-year residents. We were responsible for our own small patient load in the hospital, with close supervision and mentoring from senior trainees and the attending physician.

My medicine sub-internship was one of my favorite rotations. My supervising attending was a young, energetic faculty member, and I worked with a whip-smart resident named Tim. I remember admitting a patient with a joint infection related to intravenous drug abuse during my first night on call that month. Tim let me drain the fluid out of my patient's elbow under his supervision, my first arthrocentesis. We examined the fluid under the microscope to see the bacteria, then chose an appropriate intravenous antibiotic. In the morning, I proudly presented my case in my newly acquired medical vocabulary, including the results of our blood tests and microscopic findings, to the attending and the rest of the team. When we entered the patient's room, we found him in good spirits, his joint pain relieved and his fever down. It felt like I'd suddenly cracked a code, like everything lined up and made sense.

I loved the challenge and the responsibility of having my own patients, and I regularly went above and beyond the requirements, staying later than necessary to talk to my patients, reading up on their diseases and treatments, and helping the residents with the menial tasks referred to as scutwork, like drawing blood and scheduling radiology studies for the patients.

By then, I had deduced that the more time you spent in the hospital, the more you learned. I also had gleaned that if I wanted the residents and attendings to treat me as deserving of their time and attention, I had to show extra initiative. I heard them talk about students who were "lazy" or "weren't dedicated," or even worse, "not Penn material," implying the med school had made a mistake when admitting them. If I stuck around, even if it meant no dinner or less sleep, the residents would share what they knew, and might even let me perform procedures under their watchful eyes. I'd also be rewarded with a glowing evaluation at the end of the month.

I was a bit brainwashed already. I'd bought into the ethic of overwork, the myth of tireless dedication. I didn't see anything wrong with staying up all night and working through the next day. I didn't see anything wrong with missing meals or waiting for three hours when I needed to use the bathroom, or not seeing my friends for weeks and months on end. The people I admired had done it, so I would, too.

Medical training, of course, does not end with graduation from medical school. There is postgraduate training, known as residency, that one must complete before becoming an attending doctor who is able to practice without supervision. Depending on the specialty one enters, that training may be completed in two years, or it may take much longer. It seemed like there were students who became jaded early, by the end of medical school, but most of us back in those days were still enthusiastic and idealistic as we entered residency training. We'd all heard residency was tough and had steeled ourselves. Still, we had no idea what we were really in for over the next few years.

For me, the three years of my Internal Medicine residency were a whirlwind of exhaustion and exhilaration, successes and failures, a bumpy ride from ignorance to mastery. I'd chosen a rigorous academic residency program in order to get both breadth and depth of experience, and I got just that. We saw just about everything during our training, from typical adult degenerative illnesses to heroin overdoses, from asthma exacerbations to the most unusual and esoteric of diseases. We carried heavy loads of seriously ill patients; the program had high expectations of its residents. My clinical training was trial by fire.

I was on call every two or three nights, except during the few months when I was assigned to the Emergency Department. On call essentially meant working in the hospital from 7 a.m. one day to 7 p.m. the next day, often with no sleep at all. During the months of Emergency Room training, I worked rotating twelve-hour day and night shifts. In all rotations, we usually had one day off per week, but sometimes it was less. I came to think of this as normal.

Looking back, I wonder if it was youth, adrenaline, or sheer will that got me through.

Maybe it was all three. What I came to accept as necessary and normal was, in retrospect, a form of insanity. Nobody can reasonably work more than thirty-six hours at a stretch with no sleep and remain at the peak of mental performance. Nobody can witness the critical illnesses and injuries we did, experience deaths on a daily basis, without registering some amount of psychological trauma. And I think very few of us truly had the steel nerves required to learn invasive procedures and management of massive bleeding and impending cardiorespiratory failure by the "see one, do one, teach one" method, as we were often forced to do.

I remember placing central lines, large-bore IVs threaded into the internal jugular vein in the neck, the tip reaching the right atrium of the heart; or pacemakers, inserted similarly, blindly at the bedside as a medical resident. I was usually successful at such procedures, but performing them terrified me. I worried, reasonably, about accidentally piercing the adjacent artery, causing blood to spurt out of the patient, or about improper pacer placement leading to a deterioration of cardiac rhythm rather than an improvement. Somehow, I stopped my hands from shaking during the insertion, but invariably, I would shake and feel nauseated after I finished. Medical residents no longer perform these procedures in most hospitals; specially trained surgeons or radiologists do them under ultrasound guidance.

During almost every night on call, when the attending doctors had gone home for the night, there would be at least one code blue, and sometimes several in a night. We, the medical residents, were in charge of running the codes, assessing life-threatening heart rhythms, administering cardiac drugs, inserting a breathing tube in the patient if necessary, hoping to reverse what were often irreversible, disastrous processes. Many of the patients we coded died, and whoever took charge of calling the shots during the code had to decide when it was time to call it, to declare the patient dead. Afterward, one of us would phone the family and deliver the bad news. The rest of us walked away, returning to our other tasks without dropping a beat.

If the patient happened to have been one of the patients I was primarily responsible for, I would be the one to call a family member. I'd sit behind the nurses' station and search the chart for the emergency contact information. Then I'd dial the phone number, never knowing what kind of reaction to expect. I'd think about whether the death was expected or completely unexpected and try to sculpt the right words out of the amorphous mass of consolations and platitudes and explanations I'd heard delivered in the past.

"Is this Mrs. Smith? Mrs. Smith, this is Dr. Kaplan at Temple Hospital. I'm so sorry to tell you that your husband suffered a cardiac arrest tonight. We performed CPR and administered drugs to stabilize his heart rhythm, but in the end, we were unable to revive him."

Sometimes the response would be a quiet, "Thank you," and a

query of next steps.

Sometimes there would be an animal sound, a moan or scream, at the other end of the phone. Occasionally, a flurry of questions. Once or twice, an accusation. No matter what the response, these phone calls shook me. I couldn't see Mrs. Smith's eyes, offer her a hug or a tissue, hold her hand. The cold anonymity glared at me when I looked in the mirror later.

One night, I was managing a middle-aged male patient with late-stage cancer. He seemed stable early in the evening but after midnight became short of breath and his blood pressure dropped precipitously. He had no "Do Not Resuscitate" order; he had asked that all possible treatments be employed to keep him alive. He went downhill so quickly his family was unable to get to the hospital before he died, despite the prolonged code we ran. I was sad and angry he had died alone in the hospital, doctors he hardly knew pumping on his chest. There was such violence to it all. I cried at the nurses' station, one of my colleagues standing next to me.

"There was nothing more you could have done," Jeff said to me.

"I know, but it was such an awful situation. He was frightened and he suffered at the end," I replied.

"Stuff happens. People die. You need to move on."

"I will. Just not in this exact moment." I said it in a whisper. I don't think Jeff heard me.

We moved on every day without allowing ourselves to process the suffering of the patients, the families. We crossed the patients who didn't make it off our lists and kept going. There was always more work to do. We were supposed to close off our hearts. I'm glad I couldn't always do that.

It was easier to ignore suffering when the suffering was my

own. Like the other residents, I worked when I was sick and when I was hungry and when I was tired. If I felt resentful, I reminded myself that others were worse off than me. Not just the patients, but sometimes other doctors, too.

One night on call, I encountered one of the male medical residents in the hallway outside the emergency room. It was close to midnight. He was pale and sweaty and appeared more acutely ill than many of the patients who were on my inpatient service. We both stopped for a moment, standing in the long, vinyl-tiled hallway with harsh fluorescent light bouncing off our white coats and pale blue scrubs.

"Doug, what's wrong?" I asked him. "You don't look well."

"I'm in PAT, apparently. I put myself on a monitor in the E.R. because I was having palpitations." PAT is short for paroxysmal atrial tachycardia, a recurrent rapid heartbeat that can be brought on by a number of factors, including stress and caffeine. The increased rate causes the heart to pump less efficiently overall, causing lowered blood pressure, dizziness, and shortness of breath.

"Well, what are you doing now? Why aren't you still hooked up to that monitor and getting treatment?" I was worried that he was up and walking around given how he looked. No doubt the stress of a night on call and the strong, bitter cafeteria coffee we all drank to help us get through the long work hours were contributing to his arrhythmia.

"I'll be fine. I'm on call for red team. We have a lot of admissions, and a few really sick patients. My intern needs my help," Doug told me.

"No way! You shouldn't be working! Call the chief resident and get somebody in to cover for you before you pass out!"

"It's midnight already. I don't want to wake anyone up. Anyway, this will probably go away on its own."

"Give me your patient list. I'll help your intern." I already had more work than I could do, but between all the residents on call that night, we'd manage to get Doug's work done, too. As hard as medical training was, we always had each other's backs when someone was in trouble.

"Thanks, but I'm going to stick it out. If I get worse, I'll let you know or call the chief."

On one hand, I thought Doug was crazy. On the other, I know I would have done the same thing. The brainwashing was complete by second year of residency. No complaining. No sick days. No overt emotions. No admissions of weakness. Don't ask for help. If you don't know the answer, look it up. Only call your superiors as a last resort.

By the end of the third year of residency, I felt fully independent and ready to be in charge. I was officially an attending doctor, able to teach other trainees and do my work without supervision. Of course, this didn't mean I knew everything. Rather, it meant I knew most of what I needed to in order to care for medical patients and how to find out the rest, either by reading or by obtaining appropriate subspecialty consults.

Like most new attending doctors, I spent the first few years of my career trying out different practice options until I found what suited me best. For me, the best fit was working for myself in a small private practice. Another internist with whom I'd worked for a couple of years in a hospital practice joined me as my practice partner. Practicing medicine was never perfect, but within our little office, we were able to do a good job. A human being answered the phone. Our tiny staff helped us to stay on top of patient calls and medication refills. Sick patients were able to get prompt appointments. Our patients were almost always satisfied with their care. They trusted us and valued our judgment. We felt good about the care we provided.

I practiced in a way that is now looked at as "old school." I didn't have my patients undress until after we'd talked and established what we needed to accomplish in a visit. We talked in my office, the patient on the loveseat or comfortable chair, before entering the exam room, which gave the patients a sense of comfort and safety. I had a print of the Physician's Prayer of Maimonides on the wall of my office: *In the Sufferer, Let Me See Only the Human Being.* This was my guiding principle. I tried hard to get to know who my patients were as people and to have a good working relationship with each one.

One patient who still lives in my mind was Sue, a woman in her late thirties, married and with three little children. She came in for an urgent appointment one day, having found a small lump, like a marble, in her breast, peeking out from behind a breast implant. Later that day she underwent a mammogram and an ultrasound, and the next day a biopsy of the mass. Within a week, she was in treatment for an aggressive breast cancer, one that had already spread into her lymph nodes.

Sue lived only about a year after her diagnosis. During that time, I saw her now and then, between her appointments with her oncologist and her surgeon. I had nothing to offer but myself, and we spent her visits talking about her husband and children, and about what she knew she'd be leaving behind. Her husband, Jim, asked me to attend her funeral, and I did.

After Sue died, Jim came to see me for his own health issues and brought his aging mother to me for hers. We often talked about Sue and about the children and how they were coping. Sometimes Jim would ask my advice, parent to parent. I told him the truth—that he was doing a wonderful job as a single father and that his children would flourish with his love and the memories they held of their mother. It was this sort of mutual respect, caring, and trust that sustained me through the better part of my career.

Around 2011, we were informed of a Medicare mandate for the proficient use of electronic medical records (EMR) within the next three years. This sent our low-budget, low- tech practice into a tailspin. We tried, but ultimately closed our doors at the end of 2012, when we became aware we would soon have to choose between paying our staff, paying ourselves, and maintaining our computer hardware and software.

I remember the day I realized these years of independent practice were coming to an end.

I had arrived at work early, before the staff came in, wanting to go over our recent financial statements and the proposed maintenance contract for our electronic medical record system to see where we might be able to free up some money. I hadn't slept well; I'd been mulling over our situation all night.

I unlocked the office door and stepped into our little waiting room. It was pleasant and tidy, but the décor, with its mauve and cherry wood chairs and Formica countertops, was outdated and a little shabby, unchanged from when we opened the business in the late 1990s. The gray carpeting, with its faint pastel patterning intended to mask dirt, was obviously worn.

Looking around, I suddenly knew. We could move money around, take out a new small- business loan, or try to cut corners, but with everything we needed to keep a business going, it was just a matter of time before we'd be unable to keep up.

Independent practices were increasingly becoming a rarity by 2012. Most of the primary care doctors I knew worked for health systems. My partner and I were holdouts. Our practice had allowed us some control over our lives and careers while we raised our children, but things had changed. Over the previous year, the stress of the EMR, along with increased restrictions on medications and tests by insurers, had already started to derail our sense of control over the previous year. The staff struggled to keep up with precertification requirements for tests and prior authorizations for medicines. Rather than sink us back into deep debt, we had to admit we needed the financial and technical supports a health system could provide.

I'd kept a hand in academic medicine, teaching at one of the area medical schools as adjunct faculty while I was in private practice. This allowed me to re-enter the world of academic medicine, which seemed preferable to just working for a health system as an employed doctor. As faculty at a medical school, I could devote a half day a week to teaching, go to conferences, and also see my patients. As an employee, I would not have to worry about the operations of the practice. the EMR, or hiring and training staff. A large faction of my private practice patients was happy to come to my new academic practice. It seemed like the best course.

But there were many downsides to making such a big change. The EMR already ruled everything in clinical care in the health system, and it was the mechanism for information sharing and communication between providers at the university. In the next few years, there would be several changes of EMR systems, requiring a facility and flexibility with technology that did not come easily to me. The learning curve for use of each new EMR is steep, and knowledge of one system does not translate to knowledge of another.

There was also pressure from administrators to see as many patients as could be crammed into a day, especially new patients, who generated higher insurance payments. I amassed so many new patients every week that I couldn't fit existing patients into my schedule. My inbox on the EMR overflowed with patient call-backs, lab results, and medication refill requests. I stayed late every night seeing sick patients, writing notes, and managing my inbox. I worked from home on the weekends, and from wherever I was on vacations. Worst of all, within a few months, I felt I hardly knew my patients at all.

There were multiple doctors in my particular practice site, and we shared on-call coverage for each other by phone in the evenings and on weekends. On weekdays, though, if I was on vacation or had a day off, I had to check my own messages and handle my patients' problems, as we all had such large patient panels we didn't have time to help each other out during office hours.

The amount of time I spent at work increased dramatically as an employed doctor and faculty member. My contract stipulated I would work four days a week, but I never really had a day off, or a weekend off, even when I wasn't on call. Still, it wasn't the amount of time spent that really bothered me. Instead, it was the way in which I was spending that time that felt onerous.

Over the years, I had acquired many patients with chronic, difficult-to-treat problems. Pain syndromes, eating disorders, migraines, bad irritable bowel syndrome—these were the patients I really felt for, because unlike the patients with cancer and diabetes and heart failure, their illnesses were ill-defined, poorly understood, and had no definitive treatments.

Often these chronically suffering patients were dismissed, disbelieved, and disrespected by medical professionals. They weren't dying. They were just in pain, day after day after day, with no end in sight. Many of them were depressed, and they'd had doctors blame their symptoms on their depression. What I understood was that their depression and their other problems were interconnected, but there usually wasn't a direct causal relationship. I was very good at being with those patients, talking with them, patiently trying different treatments and modalities. In private practice, when I spent extra time at work, it was usually spent on their care.

Now, instead of spending my time with the patients who needed attention, or researching new treatments, or conferring with colleagues and specialists who might have ideas for symptoms management, I spent much of my time writing notes and orders on the computer, which took much longer than it ever took to write notes or orders on paper. Every entry in the electronic medical record required numerous clicks: clicks to log onto the computer, to log into the medical record, to identify the correct patient, to enter information, to save the information, to choose the right laboratory for a lab order or the right pharmacy for a medication order. Clicks to choose the right form of a medication, the desired dose, the number of tablets, the number of refills. Click, click, click, clickety, clickety click, click, click, click. *Oh shit, I didn't click on "save" and now I have to enter it all over again!* "Death by a thousand clicks" is a phrase every doctor I know understands all too well.

I came to know my computer screen, that impassive, brightly blinking rectangle, much more intimately than I knew the faces of my patients or my colleagues. For every hour of direct patient contact, primary care doctors now spend two hours on digital documentation and administrative tasks. We were yoked to the computer by administrators who chastised us if our charts weren't completed within twenty-four hours or if our revenues dipped or if our "metrics" (data on immunizations and other health measures) were not entered into the computer. The metrics were, in theory, to be entered by clerical staff members, but we didn't have adequate staff to stay on top of this task, so we entered the data ourselves.

An administrator in the so-called Quality department sent the doctors report cards each month that compared our performance with that of our colleagues in our own offices as well as other doctors in other offices and even in other health systems. But the report cards did not reflect the quality of our medical care or even patient satisfaction. Instead, they reflected the efficiency and thoroughness of our data entry. We were rewarded with bonuses and raises for good report cards. We were shamed for bad report cards, as our "grades" were shared with the entire health system.

Administrators seemed to be everywhere, infiltrating every aspect of the practice of medicine. They dictated our schedules, patient loads, staffing, office routines, dress codes, and codes of conduct. They had control over our computer use (and could read our emails and documents at will), our educational activities (they had to approve attendance at conferences and time spent teaching), and even aspects of our health (we were not allowed to look at our own medical charts in the EMR, for example). While I tried to view all this as the price for working for a large institution, it was hard to reconcile all the monitoring of my activities with the autonomy I'd had when I was self-employed, an autonomy we had all taken for granted on graduation from medical school. I had always held myself to very high ethical standards, so it felt particularly demeaning to have someone watching my every move.

In the last three decades, the number of physicians entering the workforce in the U.S. has had little or no growth, but the number of medical administrators has grown three thousand percent. The majority of medical administrators have no clinical experience, yet they dictate when, where, and how physicians practice medicine. Administrative costs in the U.S. are almost forty percent higher than they are in Canada; much of the expense is administrator salaries.

It wasn't only the health system that was overrun by administrators. The number of medical insurance company administrators has also risen dramatically. The health systems and insurance companies and pharmaceutical companies and pharmacies all haggle back and forth, trying to gain financial leverage over each other. One thing insurance company administrators deal with is the management of prior authorizations for medications and pre-certifications for diagnostic medical tests, policies put in place by medical insurers to prevent unnecessary utilization of resources. Management of these requests now occupies almost fifteen hours of staff and clinician time weekly for the average physician in the U.S. The financial cost to a medical practice is in the tens of thousands of dollars per physician per year. Treatment delays due to prior authorizations and pre-certifications are common, and research shows they cause some patients to abandon treatment altogether.

Often, a prior authorization or pre-certification requires a phone call to an insurance company employee. Most of those employees have no clinical background. The exception is the medical director, an insurance company employee with an M.D. degree. When a dispute over payment for a drug or test cannot be easily resolved, the patient's physician may be asked to consult with this medical director and convince him or her that the medication is necessary.

These phone calls repeatedly reminded me that just because an insurance medical director has an M.D. degree does not mean he knows anything about clinical medicine.

"Hello, this is Dr. Jones."

"Hi, Dr. Jones, this is Dr. Kaplan. I am calling because my patient's medication has been denied for payment by your company." I give him the patient information.

"Well, I see here this medication is no longer on our formulary. Has she been on three medications that are in our formulary and failed them?"

"I don't know. She has been on this medication, which is a very inexpensive generic, for twenty years, and her blood pressure and kidney function are optimal on it. She's eighty years old. It's not in her best interest to change her medication now."

"Well, we have to set limits to conserve resources. She needs to be on a formulary medication."

My fantasy is to ask this man how much money he received from the insurance company as a bonus last year, a bonus he earned by denying services for patients. Probably it was hundreds of thousands of dollars. Then I would suggest he donate two dollars a month to pay for my patient's medication, which is how much it would likely cost the insurance company. The patient is a nun who has no income and devotes all her energy to the care of at-risk children.

Instead, I persist in my argument that a change in medication will harm my patient and tell the medical director I will hold him responsible if her kidneys are damaged. Finally, after fifteen minutes, I wear him down, and he gives in. This is one of six such phone calls I will make on this day.

Administrators in health systems and in insurance companies have stake in the charges patients incur for medical services, and the EMR plays an integral part in both the charges from physicians and health systems and the actual amounts paid by the insurers. One of the reasons EMRs are so inefficient and unwieldy for clinicians is they were, in fact, developed for purposes of medical billing rather than for ease of patient care. Billing was another task that fell to us as the physicians using the EMR. Unsurprisingly, the billing function only works as well as the person using it. And there lies the rub, as medical billing is quite complicated, relying on complex algorithms. Doctors are notoriously bad at it.

At one point, I received an email from the health system's chief compliance officer informing me that some of my billing was inaccurate. Since the health system had to review every bill before it went out, it seemed like it would simplify things to have professional billers, but instead, we were required to learn to do the billing. If our coding and billing were not correct at least eighty percent of the time, there were consequences.

Apparently, I had under-coded, and thus under-billed, some charts, likely because during our compliance training, we were told over-billing is a crime. I sometimes erred on the side of caution. Now, I was being informed under-billing was also a crime.

The email stated I had been scheduled for mandatory remedial compliance training, and that if I didn't show improvement, I would be labeled an "error-prone provider." (To boot, I was also a criminal.) The phrase "error-prone provider" rattled around in my head. It was just one more indignity in a long string of indignities.

It wasn't only the billing compliance officer who was dissatisfied with various aspects of my performance. Patients were upset because they couldn't get convenient appointments, or I was running late when they arrived, or payment for their medication was denied by insurance companies. Staff complained if one of my patients was short-tempered or if my patients required too many medication refills or pre-certifications for tests, tasks the staff were responsible for managing, as if I could manipulate my patients' demeanors and limit their needs.

My increasing inability to please patients, staff, and administrators was, for me, probably one of the more painful aspects of my situation. From the time I was a child, positive external feedback served as a great motivator for me, and I consistently received it in the form of top grades in school and glowing reviews from mentors, colleagues, and patients. In this strange new world ruled by administrators and number crunchers, I was no longer getting all As on my report card. I knew I was doing the best I could, given the constraints of the system, and certainly no worse than any other doctor.

More importantly, I still had empathy for patients, and my evaluation and treatment were thorough and sound. But actual quality of care was never evaluated, and I hadn't developed the capacity to give myself credit for what I was doing right. Instead, I felt like if I tried hard enough, I should have been able to do it all—to make everyone happy. So, I just kept trying harder, running faster and faster on a road that led nowhere.

The business of medicine surely degraded the practice of medicine sufficiently to take much of the joy out of my daily professional life. But I might still be there, running in place, if I hadn't been pushed over the edge of an abyss by interpersonal problems in our practice.

Perhaps I should have known the work environment there would be toxic before I started the job when one of the doctors told me, "I just want you to know there's only one queen bee in this practice, and it's me."

I can make excuses for being naïve. For one thing, I wanted the situation to work, and I had already accepted the offer of employment when she said this. Besides, I had never encountered significant conflicts with colleagues. I rationalized that the group just wanted to make sure I was okay with not being in charge since I'd been the boss in my own practice. So, I let the comment go, and didn't let it worry me.

The association I made in my mind, though, was to *Queen Bees and Wannabes*, a book about relationships between adolescent girls—the social politics of cliques, the exclusion of girls the author refers to as "Bystanders," and the bullying of obviously vulnerable girls, known as "Targets." I dismissed the association. *"Queen Bee" is just a phrase,* I told myself. The book was about teenagers, and we were grown-up women in our forties and fifties, professionals with children.

I guess I shouldn't have tossed the idea out so readily. It soon became apparent that the social politics in my new office were far more destructive and hurtful than those of teenage cliques. They were sly and covert, and they occurred at many levels. Within a few months of my new position, my head was spinning. A physician's assistant wasn't speaking to the receptionist. Two medical assistants argued in the hallway. The nurse was angry at the office manager. One doctor thought another doctor was lazy.

As a new personality in the office, I started off as a "Bystander" to it all, but soon it was clear I was to be brought into the fray. I'd come into this office already worn down from overwork and moving my practice. I was visibly vulnerable, so I became a "Target." By the end of the year, multiple people in the office had taken issue with everything about me, from the way I said "good morning" to the font I used in my emails. One employee asserted that my standards were too high, and I asked too much of the staff. I wasn't sure how that could be true, as it seemed I was constantly performing clerical functions the staff was supposed to do but never got around to.

I felt constantly blindsided and confused. The office was chaotic; we ran perpetually behind as we were understaffed to begin with and, on top of that, someone on the staff called in sick almost every day. Phone calls were dropped, medication refill requests were not relayed to the providers, patients were scheduled improperly. Medical assistants and desk staff were late for work or absent. Once, a medical assistant quit in the middle of a patient session. When someone quit or was fired, new, untrained staff members started, so we had to constantly adjust. And I never knew when someone might try to start an argument with me.

My husband, a seasoned leader in academic medicine, offered suggestions, but when I followed them and nothing improved, he bought me a small, angry-looking plastic wildebeest.

"This will protect you," he told me. I carried it in the pocket of my white coat during patient hours and set it on my desk while I completed charts. It was my talisman. My internal mantra was, "Deploy the wildebeest."

"What is that?" asked one of the medical assistants, pointing to the plastic creature on my desk.

"A wildebeest," I replied flatly. She looked at me quizzically. I shrugged and walked away.

The practice administrators promised solutions to the problems, but none ever came. When I brought up concerns or made suggestions, I was told to "be patient" and "stop complaining." I became increasingly anxious and reactive to the point at which

I actually was, for the first time in my life, unpleasant to coworkers. At the same time, I overcompensated around the patients, not wanting them to see what a mess they had walked into. This was the place I had chosen to practice, the place I was bringing my patients to. It was humiliating.

The interpersonal problems became the fatal blow. I felt terrible about the care I was providing, about the place I worked, and, most of all, about myself. No matter how difficult things had gotten at other points in my career, even in med school and residency, I'd always known my colleagues and staff supported me. But now that was gone. When I was at work, I felt more alone than I'd ever felt in my life, an outcast child on a playground, the last kid to be picked for a team in gym class. I figured I must have deserved this in some way, but I couldn't figure out what I should have done differently.

Work was painful enough, but having no friends, no allies, made it unbearable. Medical professionals spend so much energy caring for others. How could we desert each other like this? If we didn't care for each other, who would care for us?

Rosalind Kaplan

I know I am not the only doctor who has ever walked away from what seemed like a successful medical career. In fact, I know lots of doctors who have left clinical medicine for pharmaceutical or other nonclinical jobs over the years, and others who chose early retirement. At fifty-seven, with thirty years of practice behind me, this was just another early retirement. But it wasn't what I'd planned. Five years before, I'd envisioned myself practicing at least until age sixty-eight or seventy, maybe longer.

It's all over the medical literature, the news, and social media: there is an epidemic of burnout in clinical medicine. Over half of doctors admit to symptoms of burnout. Physicians and patients agree that our medical system is broken, and everyone is suffering.

The term "burnout" was coined in the 1970s by psychologist Herbert Freudenberger to describe the consequences of severe stress and high ideals in the helping professions. The symptoms include emotional exhaustion, depersonalization, and a feeling of low personal accomplishment. It looks a lot like depression, but the symptoms have to be related to work to be called burnout.

Get this: doctors have the highest rate of suicide of any profession in the U.S. Suicide rates are higher for doctors than they are for the military, and two to four times higher than that of the general population. About four hundred doctors, the equivalent of two full medical school classes, die by suicide every year.

In the two years before I actually resigned, I had intermittently fantasied about quitting but would always put the thought aside, assuring myself it would get better, that I just wasn't trying hard enough, or I hadn't done everything I needed to do to make it work. I thought I would be sorry if I gave up the wonderful group of patients I had. There is a shortage of good primary care doctors, and I worried I would be abandoning my more vulnerable patients. I told myself we needed the income, and I didn't know how to do anything else, and that I'd invested most of my life in medicine, so I needed to continue practicing. But the truth was my heart wasn't in it.

There were even moments I contemplated killing myself. As melodramatic as it sounds, it sometimes seemed like it would be easier to die than to quit, and also easier to die than to continue. I felt like I had a debt to pay, like I owed something to medicine, and that leaving would be defaulting on that debt. I never actually came close to suicide, though. Somewhere inside, I held an image of my husband and my young adult children, my beloved dog, my kind and loving friends. Sometimes it registered there was more to my life than work.

Was I burned out? While I don't think I ever lost empathy for my patients, I suppose my choice to leave my medical practice could be attributed to burnout. I did have emotional exhaustion, and I felt like I was not accomplishing what I wanted to, which was to provide good care to my patients. I had lost all sense of joy in practicing medicine.

There are a lot of people in medicine who feel that "burnout" is the wrong term for the distress doctors are feeling in practice these days. Saying we have burnout is, in a sense, blaming the physician for the results of what are actually systemic problems. Some experts even go so far to say that the real issue is not burnout but "moral injury," comparing our situation to that of soldiers in combat who are forced to make decisions and take actions that go against their ethical convictions. This does resonate. I spent way too much time on administrative tasks and too little time with each patient, which went against my ethical convictions. I made suboptimal treatment plans for patients when the optimal treatment was not covered by insurance and too expensive for the patient to afford out-of-pocket. That, too, went against my convictions. And the fact that students and residents were not learning best practices certainly seemed immoral.

The day I walked away from my medical career, I worried I would never feel whole again. At 4 p.m. on my last day, I tossed my tote bag over my shoulder and picked up the one remaining box of books and papers perched on my otherwise barren desk. I stepped into an empty white-and-blue tiled hallway. Most of the exam room doors were closed, as the other doctors and the staff were busy seeing patients. I walked toward the waiting room, the sound of my sensible two-inch heels echoing down the hall. The two receptionists at the front desk didn't look up from their computer screens, so I didn't say goodbye. I slipped out the door to the parking garage. For a second, I panicked, knowing there was no going back. Then I remembered that I didn't want to.

Part II
Putting on New Hats

When I left primary care practice, I told people I was shedding my white coat for good. I had plans, and they did not involve a lab coat or a stethoscope. Maybe I thought at the time I'd never be in my "doctor" role again, but *working* as a doctor and *being* a doctor are not synonymous. In fact, I would continue to put on my doctor hat, if not my white coat, in an intermittent fashion, in every aspect of my life. Still, during the process of leaving my medical practice, I didn't understand that.

As excited as I was about the plans I'd made for the next couple of years, what I would be doing was starkly different than what I'd been doing for the last several decades, and that worried me. Pretty much my whole adult life, I'd been a caretaker. I took care of thousands of patients, shepherded hundreds of students. I raised my children, cared for an elderly grandmother and a dying parent.

Now, my plan was to pursue a Master's of Fine Arts (MFA) in creative writing, a goal involving no caretaking at all. The purpose of my caretaking years was clear to me: I served others. What would my purpose be in my next pursuit?

I had applied and been accepted to a writing program. Once I resigned from my job, starting that program became a reality. As it happened, the program started just two days after my last day of work, which mercifully left me little time to dwell on my dearth of purpose.

In the last days before I left work and those couple of days before the MFA program began, I told myself writing would be my new purpose, but it seemed wrong since writing is something I'd loved doing for years. I'd even managed to do it while still in medical practice. Besides, my writing had reached only a very small audience up to that point. It was great for me, but what would I be doing for others, or for my family, or for that matter, the world?

Not wanting to put the whole responsibility of supporting ourselves and helping out our fledgling adult children on my husband, I thought vaguely I'd find some kind of medical writing job while I worked on my MFA so I had some source of income. I tried reminding myself I could revisit the issue of purpose after I'd had a few months away from the daily chaos of primary care medicine. But no matter what spin I put on it, I wasn't emotionally comfortable. I couldn't shake the feeling I was doing something wrong, traveling in an errant direction.

It turned out that the beginning of the MFA, which consisted of an intensive, all-consuming residential period in Cambridge, Massachusetts, was exactly what I needed. I immersed myself in reading and writing. I made new friends who had nothing to do with medicine. I wrote what felt meaningful and true. I wrote about the patients I'd cared for, the relationships I'd formed with them. I wrote about the stresses and traumas and disappointments of my medical career. I wrote about my love for the discipline of medicine, the art and science that so captivated me, but also about my hatred for the corporate culture medical practice had become. As I wrote, I slowly began to heal. After a while, as my head cleared, I was able to write about other aspects of life.

For a month or so, I didn't think much about going back to the practice of medicine, and I didn't care that I didn't have a job. After a while, though, I saw I could do the work for the master's program and still have some time on my hands. I reached out to a contact at a medical publishing company who offered me some freelance medical writing work. Writing about medical topics wasn't all that creative, but it wasn't a bad part-time gig. Except that reading and writing about the art and science of medicine started to make me miss patient care.

I tried not to pay attention to the tug. I didn't want to go back to a primary care job with Death by a Thousand Clicks and a bottomless, life-sucking in box. But when I got a call from a company looking for a doctor in an urgent care center, I was curious. Maybe it would be different.

At first, I didn't think it was for me. I would have to read x-rays and suture wounds and take care of kids, all things I hadn't done in years. The senior physicians encouraged me to try a shift or two with help from a physician's assistant who was proficient at these tasks. It turned out that I recovered the skills very quickly. They accepted my time constraints, allowing me to do just one twelve-hour shift a week so I could still do the work for my MFA. The pay they offered was very fair, and the contract only asked me to commit for a year.

A shift in urgent care can be busy, sometimes even a little overwhelming. But it has a beginning and an end, and in between, the time goes fast. I arrive in the morning wearing a set of high-tech, wrinkle-free surgical scrubs and leather Dansko clogs. It feels like I'm in pajamas and slippers, but I look like a doctor. In fact, I look like someone who means business.

My team consists of a receptionist, an x-ray technician, a nurse, and a medical assistant. We gather in the work area—a huge, brightly lit room with a central nurse's station and multiple exam rooms around the perimeter, including one we call the crash room, which contains heart monitoring equipment, a gurney, and a cart filled with emergency medical equipment and cardiac drugs. There is also a larger, lead-lined room, in which x-rays are obtained. The space has the same configuration as an emergency room, but on a smaller scale. We lack the equipment an E.R. would have for its most critical patients, but we have much more than a typical doctor's office would.

We conduct our morning huddle, during which we assign tasks in case of a cardiac arrest or other dire emergency.

"I'll take airway management," I tell the team.

"Okay, I'm on chest compressions," says Adrienne, the nurse. "Brooke, you call 911 and set up the AED (automatic defibrillator)," she tells our receptionist.

"That leaves me to put in the intravenous line," the medical assistant volunteers.

Patient hours begin. Our first patient, who arrived before the clinic even opened, was bitten by his neighbor's cat the night before, and awoke this morning with severe pain in his hand and a red streak forming up his arm. I examine him and ask when his last tetanus shot was. He can't remember, so I order one. The wound is infected, and I ask the nurse to place an IV and order a dose of intravenous antibiotics to get prompt control over the infection. While the medical assistant cleans the bite and the nurse sets up the IV, I go talk to the next patient, a college student who's had a painful sore throat, fevers, and swollen lymph nodes for over a week, too long to be strep throat. I order a rapid test for mononucleosis, which comes up positive five minutes later. While the mono test is running and the cat bite patient gets his antibiotics,

I examine an older man with eye pain, and find a corneal abrasion and a grain of sand in his eye. I remove the sand and write a prescription for eye drops.

"Thanks, Doc," the man with the cat bite says, as he signs his discharge papers. "I don't know what I would have done if you all weren't here. I don't have a doctor, and a visit to the E.R. would have taken hours and cost thousands of dollars! I wish you could be my regular doctor."

I wish that too, just for a minute. I still miss the long-term relationships, but that kind of doctoring comes at too high of a cost to my sanity in the current medical environment.

The day progresses, and the shift is half over by the time I look up at the clock. We have a lull, and I go in the kitchen and eat my lunch, two hours later than usual. Afterward, the nurse and I will catch up on the charts; she will enter the history and log medications she gave, while I add the physical exam and treatment plan. By 9 p.m., I will have seen between twenty-five and forty patients. There will be periods in the day when I have a number of patients waiting and feel under pressure, but those stressful moments pass.

An elderly woman will complain of difficulty breathing and have an abnormal EKG, and I will transfer her to the hospital by ambulance. A child will be brought in by his father, screaming and dripping blood from a laceration, but leave smiling, holding stickers and a lollipop, after I suture his chin. I will leave at 9 p.m., wired and tired, but knowing I will have time to recover before my next shift.

Here's some more good news. I get along with everyone. There's rarely any drama or subterfuge, and there are minimal politics. Occasionally, especially since the stress of the pandemic, I encounter patients who are angry or agitated, dissatisfied by what we can offer them in an urgent care visit, but we work as a team to handle their behavior as well as their medical concerns so we can move on from any unpleasant encounters. So here I am, a "rehabilitated" burned-out doctor, doing something familiar but also novel, something that works for me for the time being. Something that feels like purpose.

Many of the patients I see in urgent care are there because they can't get an appointment to see their own doctors when they are sick. Some are there because they have no medical insurance, and we offer a lower fee structure for an out-of-pocket visit than most doctor's offices do. Not infrequently, patients come to us when they are really sick—the kind of sick that requires a hospital emergency department, but they are afraid of an E.R. bill, and hope we can help them.

Sometimes we can. If we must transfer them to an E.R., we do, but we understand their fear. These situations remind me daily of how broken our medical system is, how desperately change is needed.

There are some aspects of medicine that have improved over the years since I first entered the field. The abuse of medical students is no longer acceptable—anyone who calls a med student names or throws surgical instruments will surely be reported by students who are empowered to advocate for themselves and disciplined by leadership who uphold academic standards. Interns and residents no longer work thirty-six hours at a stretch, and there is much closer supervision of medical decisions and procedures by trainees after errors related to inexperience and overwork were reported by the press in the 1980s.

Despite these changes, depression and despair among medical students and residents are rampant. The acuity of illness in hospitalized patients is much higher, and admissions are much shorter than they were a couple of decades ago. Patient turnover is fast and furious, putting tremendous pressure on resident physicians. Students, too, are under pressure. The cost of medical school in the U.S. has soared, and the average debt of a student graduating from med school as of 2021 was just above $200,000. These young doctors-to-be also see suffering and death on a daily basis, and often incur secondary trauma, even with mechanisms now in place to try to mitigate those effects.

Change never seems to come to medicine easily. It has been much slower than it ought to be, with many growing pains. I can only hope the changes will bring better health not only for patients, but also for doctors and other healthcare workers.

My MFA, as it turned out, has served some tangible purpose beyond the time and structure to write, and even beyond the ability to write well enough to touch more readers. I am also able now to teach the craft of writing, and I've chosen to teach it to medical students. One of the Philadelphia area medical schools hired me to teach within their humanities program. Such programs didn't exist when I was a medical student or resident, but in attempts to both improve patient satisfaction and also prevent physician burnout, many us medical schools now have instruction in the arts—writing, visual arts, music, even dance—with an emphasis on the intersection of humanism and medicine.

Many writing classes within medical education focus on writing about patient stories, something we call "narrative medicine," as a way to understand the patient as a whole person who lives in the world rather than just as a sick person. While there is much inherent value in this, I choose instead to encourage the students to write about themselves, reflecting on their own pasts and musing about their futures. I hope this will lead to a practice of writing for well-being for this group of students as they move forward. I hope it will help them process the joys, sorrows, fears, and frustrations of medical training and practice so the hard times are less likely to lodge inside them as traumas. I also hope that by sharing their personal writing in class, by taking that risk, they will learn to share the feelings with their colleagues throughout their careers, no matter how frightening or difficult those feelings might be.

In one of my classes, a student writes about losing a loved one, and the painful emotions cadaver dissection elicited for her. After she reads her writing, another student speaks up.

"I wish I'd known you were struggling. We didn't really know each other then, but I was right at the next dissection table. I would have held your hand."

During another semester, one of the men reflects in an essay on how awkward he felt approaching his very first patient, and how confident all the other students seemed in comparison. Several of his classmates nod and smile as he reads.

"That's exactly how I felt!" another student says. "I thought I was the only one!"

Each group has entered the writing class as acquaintances, if not strangers, but they leave as trusted friends. I believe in our writing exercises as part of the way forward in medical culture, a piece I wish I'd had much earlier in my career, something I now feel good about bringing to my profession.

I will never say I regret practicing medicine or that I regret my time as a primary care doctor. Taking care of patients has always felt like a privilege. In my career, thousands of people have trusted me with their health, their lives, their emotional well-being, and their deepest feelings. Those people believed in me. Hundreds of my patients followed me as I moved from one practice to another. They supported me, not just financially, but professionally through their trust, and emotionally through deep bonds we built over years of working together. Those bonds were magical and irreplaceable.

When I left practice, many of my patients told me that while they would miss me, they were glad I was finally going to take care of myself. A number of them contacted me after I left, even though I'd made sure each patient had a new doctor to see. They weren't calling for medical advice, but because they just wanted to chat. The bonds didn't necessarily die with the end of our doctor-patient relationship. Now, several years later, I still talk to a number of my former patients. A few have become dear friends, and I feel especially honored by those friendships.

I'm healing now. I'm not done with medicine, and it's not done with me. My contributions to medicine are different, but they have value. I still have something to give, and now I am being nourished in return. Writing, my patients, and my students are healing me.

ELEVEN

A Diary of Calamities

1. November 2019, Foreshadow

On a Friday evening, a forty-five-year-old woman named Maria was driving her Subaru Forester along a Pennsylvania highway about fifteen miles away from Philadelphia. It was raining heavily. She drove more slowly than she ordinarily would, partly due to poor visibility, but also because the wind seemed unusually strong, which forced her to keep her hands firm at ten and two on the vinyl steering wheel, so as not to allow the vehicle to be blown about the road.

Maria was just about to change the car radio station from the usual alternative rock to local news, hoping to hear a weather report, when she saw the cyclone cloud headed directly toward her.

Before she could do anything other than draw in a sharp, curtailed breath, she found herself levitated above the highway by a powerful upward force. The second or two she spent suspended in the atmosphere stretched out in her consciousness and expanded in an arc over what seemed the entire earth. She wondered if this was what death actually felt like—a shocked eternity, purgatory above an expressway.

But eventually, her car slammed back down to the ground, tires again contacting the asphalt, now turned nearly 180 degrees around so that it faced the direction from which she'd come.

Maria discovered she was alive, unbroken, though not unharmed. All her limbs, her fingers and toes, moved on her mental command. Shaking, she opened the car door and stepped out onto the highway and into an eerie quiet.

I meet Maria the next day, when she limps in the urgent care center where I am working a hectic Saturday shift. She tells me she feels a bit dazed. She isn't sure if she hit her head during the incident, but what hurts the most is her right hip and thigh, which slammed into the driver's side door while she was whirling in the sky.

My evaluation reveals evidence of a mild concussion, whiplash, and a large bruise reaching from hip to knee. I order x-rays to rule out hip or femur fracture. Beyond that she is still in a bit of shock, terrified by her bizarre encounter with the whims of nature.

While I wait for the radiology technician to complete Maria's x-rays, I document her encounter on the electronic medical record and complete the billing form by entering her ICD-10 diagnosis codes, the numerical codes assigned to each patient problem by the International Classification of Diseases, the bible of medical coding. The codes all live in part of the electronic medical record program, so I enter the diagnoses, and the program generates the code numbers. Concussion without Loss of Consciousness, initial encounter—S06.0X1A. Contusion of Right Thigh, initial encounter—S70.11XA.

Oh, right, I'm supposed to mention the mechanism of injury. The ICD-10 has codes for just about everything. In the past, I've coded for Fear of Chickens, F40.218, and Bitten by Pig W55.41. There's even a code for Burned by Water Skis on Fire, V91.07X, so it's not surprising that there'd be one for Tornado, initial encounter—X37.1XXA. Yes, there is a code for Tornado. I just thought I'd never have to use it.

Maria's x-rays show no signs of a fracture. She leaves satisfied that the physical injuries will heal in time. She is less certain how to handle her post-traumatic fear.

I feel afraid, too, after her visit. The fact that I, an urgent care doctor in a suburb of Philadelphia, am coding for "Tornado, initial encounter" is deeply disturbing. It is only in the last few years that tornadoes have become a thing in the Philadelphia area. They used to hit once in a decade; now, it's not unusual to hear tornado warnings on the local news. Is this the new normal, coding for injuries from weather disasters here in Pennsylvania?

I guess it's good the ICD-10 is prepared, but I don't think anyone else is.

2. March, 2020 – Calamity, Take One

Nobody is ready for the disaster we have come to call Coronavirus Disease 2019, or COVID-19. Even the ICD-10 is not ready this time. We start out using existing code U07.1, Other Viral Pneumonia, and stick "COVID-19" onto the end of it as a suffix. It doesn't take long to figure out that this disease is like no other we have encountered. It will soon have its very own set of billing codes.

The day we learn that Pennsylvania is going into lockdown

because of COVID is a Friday. Friday the 13th to be exact, though the irony of that doesn't register at the time.

I am sitting in Starbucks with my friend Kate.

"This will be the last Friday coffee together for a while," Kate says. "I wonder how long it will be. Are you worried?"

"I don't know. I mean, yes. I've never seen anything like this, but I have to believe we will be okay."

In fact, Kate and I won't see each other again for months; there will be no sitting in cafes or bars or restaurants, no social gatherings, beginning on Monday, March 17, 2020, and lasting... indefinitely.

The weekend before lockdown, Larry and I go to the grocery store. So does everyone else. There are no frozen items on the shelves, and toilet paper is already scarce. We buy the last potato in the produce department. We are social distancing, staying six feet from other people, washing our hands a hundred times a day.

Some people are washing their groceries before bringing them into their homes, wearing rubber gloves to open their mail and packages. I can't convince myself I need to do this. I will be careful, as I would with a cold or flu epidemic, not to touch my face, my mouth, my eyes.

I do want hand sanitizer, and there is none of that to be found. I find a recipe for homemade sanitizer. It calls for rubbing alcohol and aloe gel. I have alcohol, but I visit four pharmacies before I find aloe gel. Then I put the ingredients into a big pot on my stove and stir, a witch stirring her poison brew.

Early in lockdown, I sit on my patio surveying my surroundings. Nobody out, it seems, not now, at three p.m. on a chilly March day. The sky is that cobalt-blue of a late winter afternoon, and wispy clouds are shifting in the wind. Suddenly, my next-door neighbor's big black dog comes bounding into my yard. He is young and spirited and apparently has escaped their fence. Behind him is my neighbor, Laura. She runs after the dog, who has now stopped and is letting me pet him. But Laura stops short, and we stare at each other. We are suddenly threats to each other. We must stay six feet away—two yardsticks, the length of a cow, the height of a taller-than-average man is the "safe" distance between humans. Too far for a gentle touch or a casual hug.

I push the dog towards Laura. She lures him with a treat and attaches his leash. We look at each other again, sigh and wave wistfully. She retreats to her yard with her dog.

I am an essential worker. I'm *essential*. I'm *needed*. Also, I'm *at risk*. Exempt from the rules of lockdown, at least when it comes to my workdays. I continue to go to work in the urgent care center.

At first, it's eerily quiet in the clinic. Nobody wants to be exposed to other people. We see ear infections, abscesses, the occasional bleeding laceration from a kitchen knife—the kind of things you really can't ignore because blood is dripping from a hand, or a child is screaming. Meanwhile, people are staying home with serious problems like chest pain and uncontrolled high blood pressure. They've been told to stay out of emergency rooms and they're afraid to seek help.

Soon we begin seeing people with fevers and coughs and loss of taste, the classic symptoms of the first version of COVID. We stick swabs up noses, send patients with low oxygen levels to the E.R., where many are admitted and some need mechanical ventilation.

When we see patients with symptoms of COVID-19, we wear PPE—Personal Protective Equipment—including N95 masks to filter out virus particles and yellow isolation gowns to prevent droplets of fluid from reaching our skin. We don't have enough masks or gowns to change them between patients, as intended. We reuse them until they disintegrate. Our hospital network, the U.S. healthcare system, and the government are all unprepared.

We don and doff our PPE in proper order. Wash hands, gown on, then mask, then eye protection, then gloves. Gown and gloves off together, without being turned inside out. Then eye protection off, then mask, and wash hands. We keep our gowns and masks in paper bags; plastic will not allow any moisture to dry and may cause growth of viruses, bacteria, and molds. Because we really don't know much about how the virus is transmitted at this point, we are always afraid of contaminating ourselves or our environment.

Arriving home after a shift at urgent care, I leave my leather clogs outside the door. I rip off my surgical scrubs just inside the door, and Larry delivers them to the laundry room, puts them in the washer on hot. I shower and wash my hair before I touch him. I am afraid for myself, but more afraid for him, because he has asthma which can make a case of COVID more deadly.

It is only the beginning, but at this point, we have no idea how long this crisis will last. A year from now, we will know more. A year from now, we will have codes for suspected COVID-19 and proven COVID-19 and pneumonia from COVID and bronchitis from COVID. More and more codes will be added as we come to know the damage the virus can do. Multisystem Inflammatory Syndrome related to COVID-19. Post-COVID Cardiomyopathy. Post-COVID Condition, unspecified. Unvaccinated for COVID and Vaccinated for COVID. The disease is a moving target, and new information will cause us to revise our treatment and prevention strategies almost daily. Still, we won't know enough.

August 2020- Calamity Take Two

My son, Max, and his wife, Kara, live in Santa Cruz, California where Max is working on his Ph.D. in Linguistics at the University of California Santa Cruz (UCSC). Santa Cruz is on fire. Fires have been common in California seemingly forever, but in recent years, the fires are more frequent and burn more acreage. Santa Cruz is a beach town, less treed and more humid than many other areas in the state, so it tends to be spared. But this summer, lightning strikes during a heat wave during a long dry period which starts a series of fires that rage in the Santa Cruz mountains. Known as the Lightning Complex fires, redwoods, brush, and then vineyards are destroyed, and it's now encroaching on the UCSC campus. The campus has been evacuated. Campus residents have been encouraged to shelter on the beach.

Max and Kara don't live on campus, but they are close by. Their go-bags, the luggage containing emergency supplies that Californians are told to keep at hand, are in the car.

They have a full tank of gas and are ready to drive away at any moment. Finally, the smoke is thick enough and the threat seems high enough that they leave, though they have not yet been ordered to evacuate. Nobody can say how long this will last.

They are lucky to have a car so they can leave town. But there's nowhere for them to go because of the pandemic. They won't impose themselves on friends or family because of the risk they might be carrying asymptomatic COVID infections.

Then, a stroke of luck. Larry's brother and sister-in-law, who live outside San Francisco in an area that has some smoke but is not under the threat of fire, will be staying at a rented house in

Lake Tahoe. Max and Kara can stay at their home for a few days.

Swathes of smoke from California have spread to the Northeast and even as far as Europe. The haze is visible. There are warnings for people with lung disease. Risk of exacerbation of asthma J45.901. Exposure to smoke, fire and flames, X01.

Max and Kara return to their home in Santa Cruz after a week, when the fire threat to the city proper has passed, but wildfires continue to rage for months in the area. The Lightning Complex fires alone burn almost 400,000 acres before they are contained. Even years later, we will not know the true health consequences of the smoke from that summer and the ones that follow.

December, 2020 — A Moment of Reprieve

I cry when I get my first COVID vaccine, just for a minute. Not from pain, but from relief, because I won't feel under constant threat of severe illness or death when I go to work. The data is solid that the vaccine decreases the risk drastically. One of my colleagues has just been released after hospitalization for COVID, and another almost died a few weeks earlier.

As a frontline worker, I receive a dose of vaccine from the very first batch available to the hospital system. I had to drive over an hour for my shot, but I don't mind at all. There is a little bit of a party atmosphere in the large conference area where we sit for thirty minutes, chairs positioned six feet from each other as we wait. We are grateful for the vaccine and for being together, even if just for a few minutes.

Rosalind Kaplan
February 2021 — Calamity, Take Three

My daughter lives in Austin, Texas with her partner. They moved there from the northeast for the lower housing costs and warmer climate. But now they're freezing. Several severe winter storms have swept through Texas, and Austin is covered in snow and ice. The unregulated Texas electrical grid has led to widespread power outages. Maddy and Ian have no electricity, no heat, and no potable water. They are both sick, possibly with COVID. Their apartment is frigid. A battery-powered charger is allowing them phone service, and they've texted us a photo of Maddy standing in the living room in multiple layers of clothing topped by her winter parka. The wall behind her is coated with ice.

The roads are impassable; Austin was not prepared for this kind of weather. Though a few friends have electricity, they can't impose on anyone when they may be contagious. They'll have to stick it out until the power returns.

I text back, asking if they have food, whether they have a way to boil water.

Maddy texts back.

We are okay. Someone dropped some bottles of water off. We have canned food. Don't worry.

I wish I could refrain from worrying. There is no way to help them from a distance, and no way to go there.

During this massive failure of Texas' power grid, at least two hundred and forty-six people will die from exposure or accidents related to lack of electricity, heat, and water. Hypothermia, initial encounter, ICD-10 code T68.XXXA. T58.14XA—toxic effect of carbon monoxide from utility gas, initial encounter. E86.0- dehydration.

Maddy and Ian are lucky. They're miserable for a few days, but they are not harmed. They have warm clothes and an intact roof. They are young and strong, and they are savvy enough to know not to make a potentially fatal error like turning the gas stove on for heat. Still, if our privileged, educated kids are in this much peril from a winter storm in a major us city, it seems delusional to believe anyone is safe.

December 2021 — Calamity, Continued

In the very early stages of the COVID pandemic, in the beginning of lockdown and the terrible surge of deaths in New York City, in the first days of grief and confusion, people were kind to each other. We were all in the same crisis, all frightened but also a little bit energized. Healthcare workers were heroes, and people banged pots to show their appreciation.

I can't say for sure when I noticed the shift from "We're all in this together" to "Every man (and woman) for him(her)self," from making hand-sewn masks for our neighbors to punching security guards who enforced masking policies, from worshipping healthcare heroes to accusing doctors and nurses of heresy. I've asked my friends and family when they noticed the change, and nobody can agree. Was it a month in, or was it a year? Our memories are hazy and vague.

Now, we are all so tired. Not just healthcare workers, but, it seems, the world. Humanity. Tired and irritable. Brittle. Waiting for the next assault on our feelings, our hopes, our values. Ready to snap and bracing ourselves to be snapped at.

In my medical microcosm, I see the destruction. Many healthcare workers, afraid of getting sick, exhausted from overwork, or traumatized by witnessing suffering and death, have retired early or found other kinds of work. This has left facilities direly understaffed, leading to more burnout of those left behind. Not to mention that we are no longer anyone's heroes. Now, it seems like patients are skeptical of diagnoses, of treatments, of preventative care. Some are even combative or frankly abusive.

"I don't want to be tested for COVID," one patient in urgent care with fever and cough tells me. He'd taken a long car trip with a group of people. Three of the five were now ill, and none have been tested for COVID.

"You have COVID symptoms. It's in your best interest to know whether you have it. It's also important for the people you traveled with to know," I say, trying to appeal to logic.

"That's why I don't want to be tested. I'm not telling other people I might have given them COVID. And I can't stay home for ten days! I have things to do!"

Another patient, a sixty-eight-year-old in my primary care clinic says, "I'm not going to get the vaccine because I don't need it. I never get sick. My immune system is superior. Getting a useless vaccine is messing with something that is working fine. Why would I do that?"

"Even if you have an excellent immune system, your body has never been exposed to this particular virus, which means it is not set up to fight off this virus. The vaccine has been given to hundreds of millions of people. There's no evidence that it will damage your immune system. COVID, on the other hand, can damage every organ system in your body," I reply, trying to dispel myths and illogical thinking.

"That's what you say, but I've read reports that say differently. The articles in a lot of the science journals you read have left out important information and covered up the truth. I'm not going to be brainwashed by you doctors."

I wonder why this patient is even here in my clinic if that's the way he feels about doctors. He has been coming to clinic twice a year for at least a decade, to have his blood pressure measured and his antihypertensive medication refilled. He takes his blood pressure medication daily, exercises regularly, and watches his salt intake, which years of research have shown to be the best way to manage hypertension. He got his routine tetanus shot and a shingles vaccine at his last visit, yet he shuns the researchers and clinicians who study the prevention and treatment of COVID. I point this out, but he tells me he's not willing to discuss COVID with "someone like me." I change the subject, and we complete our visit.

I am not insulted by his vaccine refusal, but I am frustrated and confused by the contradictions. Why is COVID different from the thousands of other conditions scientists and doctors diagnose, treat, and try to prevent? Why are patients accepting false data about this potentially fatal disease, often while following mainstream recommendations around their other medical conditions?

If this man contracts COVID and becomes seriously ill, I'm sure he'll come to the hospital looking for treatment. And he will receive it—including the medications and mechanical supports science and medicine have developed through rigorous study protocols—treatments that have the capacity to save his life.

Every man for himself. Every woman for herself. The argument that we should each make our own decisions about our own bodies is a fraught one. When it comes to communicable disease, the decisions we make are not just about our own well-being, they affect everyone. A social contract would mean we might have to make some concessions to help the community, the nation, or the world. Sadly, what we've seen around COVID is that we lack a strong social contract. Perhaps we have no social contract at all.

In truth, lack of agreement regarding personal versus societal well-being had already placed the U.S. healthcare system on a path to failure well before COVID reared its head. The refusal to take data seriously has been with us throughout time. Data shows that, despite much higher costs, the health of the U.S. population lags behind that of other industrialized, wealthy countries, all of which have national health systems. The American resistance to "socialism," an emotional, knee-jerk reaction to semantics, has left us in the dust and created a complicated, piecemeal system that leaves large swaths of U.S. citizens without access to prevention or treatment, leaves healthcare workers burned out and frustrated, and increases racial and socioeconomic disparities. Inadequate funds have been allocated to public health for decades, contributing to a weakened response to COVID, the biggest threat to our way of lives in over a century.

The American Medical Association just published a study stating that one in five doctors and two in five nurses intends to leave clinical practice within the next two years. Add to this an aging population requiring more care, and a new crisis is indeed brewing. The factors driving the intent to leave practice were reported as high levels of burnout, stress, workload, fear of infection, and COVID-19 related depression and anxiety. The study authors concluded that "reducing burnout and improving a sense of feeling valued may allow healthcare organizations to better maintain their workforces post-pandemic."

I feel sad and discouraged reading this. I'm pretty sure the horse is out of the barn. I doubt our ability to dig out of this without restructuring our whole medical system. There is no health in our healthcare system. It doesn't care for health. Prevention isn't lucrative. In a capitalist system, payment for treatment of illness is what pays. What we have is a fragmented system for sick care, and that's not working either. The system itself is sick, and there's no ICD-10 code for that.

March, 2023 — Quieter Calamities?

We've had a suspiciously warm winter so far in Philadelphia. No snow at all. I usually wouldn't wish for snow, but it all seems wrong. Meanwhile, San Bernardino County in Southern California is in a snow emergency, with over ten feet of snow trapping people in their homes and causing buildings to cave in, a situation never seen before.

Larry and I both had our first and only case of COVID in January, after traveling, but the community level of the virus has been relatively low this month. It's easy for me to tell when the case numbers are rising; I'll see an increase in positive tests in urgent care clinic almost immediately. Nobody talks much about COVID anymore, but a recent wedding I was invited to but didn't attend was reportedly a "super-spreader" event—a large group of guests became ill in the few days after the reception.

Our patient volume in urgent care is way up, but not because of COVID. It seems to me more people are bringing all their problems—acute and chronic medical problems, mental health crises, preventative health needs—to urgent care. Many don't have primary care doctors, and it is extremely difficult to get an appointment with a primary care doctor as a new patient. There are also the uninsured patients who hope we can take care of everything in a single, relatively inexpensive visit.

I'm not working full-time in urgent care, and my teaching demands are light. While I sometimes feel stress during a busy shift, I don't feel chronically stressed or burned out. I have time to exercise, eat meals, socialize, and sit with feelings. At this late stage of my career, I have that luxury, but I recognize it as a luxury. Many of my friends and colleagues in medicine are feeling overwhelmed and some are in despair, feeling they have no control over their daily lives.

We're talking about it more. On physician blogs, you see posts about burnout and stress regularly. Some of the professional societies offer counseling and continue to advocate for change. Still, I don't see much change at an institutional level. Healthcare organizations offer yoga classes and mindfulness meditation at lunchtime or after work, though doctors are working through lunch and are already away from home too much to stay after work. One professional organization just sent out a flyer about a program to help medical professionals "reframe" their stress. But where are the efforts to decrease the stress in the first place? Doctors are still being told to fix themselves, despite the fact that the problem is a broken system.

What Calamities?

A few hundred people are still dying from COVID every day in the U.S. Many people who get the current iteration of COVID say it's not worse than a cold, but it is the deadliest respiratory virus in current circulation.

We mostly behave like there's no pandemic. We go out to eat, we go shopping without a mask, we go to weddings and funerals. Does that mean we've forgotten about it?

I'm sure some people have just put COVID aside as something that happened and is over. I haven't. As a healthcare worker, I have to think of risk all the time. What's the risk that this patient has COVID? If he does, what's the risk he'll become seriously ill? What's the risk that I'll contract COVID at this wedding or on this train? Is the benefit worth the risk for me?

I think we'd all like to forget the intense fear and chaos, and the financial, social, and emotional fallout of COVID. But forgetting means we won't take anything away from the collective experience. It means wasting all the knowledge and wisdom available to us.

The devastation of COVID should have made us aware of how vulnerable we all are. New infectious diseases are always popping up, and we need to prepare for the next pandemic, which experts say is just about inevitable. A healthy response would mean bolstering our public health infrastructure, stockpiling necessary medical and protective equipment, and educating the population in advance of the next public health crisis. Instead, public health measures remain vastly underfunded. When a surge of Monkey Pox (now called MPox) emerged in 2022, we were at sea almost immediately, even though tests and treatments already existed. We just weren't prepared to use them to best advantage. It makes me wonder when we're going to wake up.

Regarding our preparation for pandemics, Dr. Tom Frieden, a former director of the Centers for Disease Control (CDC), said in a 2021 CNN article, "We are at risk of heading full steam ahead into the neglect phase of the panic-neglect cycle." We panic in the face of immediate threat and then, when the crisis passes, we fall into complacency and ennui, and we neglect to prevent the next, similar crisis. It comes, we panic again, and the cycle repeats itself.

It seems like it's not just infectious disease that elicits the panic-neglect cycle. It's also climate disasters and hate crimes, gun violence and economic disparities ,and mental health crises. It's the crumbling of a healthcare system, though with climate crisis and pandemic, good medical care is more necessary than ever before. We panic and mobilize briefly, and then move on to the next distraction. Each calamity is dropped into a big pot, where it simmers in a bitter brew, waiting to boil over. Inside that cauldron, these societal ills become inextricable. Climate change creates opportunities for new infectious diseases and illness leading to economic hardship, which then feeds the spate of gun violence, further stressing a wounded healthcare system already plagued with racial disparity . . . and so on, an infinite cycle.

I worry that with each new calamity, people will become more and more inured to crisis, or more and more fatalistic, to the point that we are paralyzed. I fear that with each failure to pass legislation to protect society, we will feel more and more helpless and finally stop trying to effect change. Most of all, I worry we will forget not just that societal systems are interdependent, but that we humans are also interdependent.

If climate disaster and disease and economic hardship and violence create a negative spiral, can't conservation and good healthcare and improving economy and a sense of responsibility for one another create a positive one? If we don't live in a healthy society, we are all at risk. But if there's fundamental disagreement on how to create a healthy society, how can a positive cycle begin? If it's "each man for himself," we all end up in the eye of the storm.

It's too much to look at all at once, a cyclone cloud threatening to pull me into the darkening sky, spin me around, and slam me back down. What can I do? I'm just one person. I break it down, react to the smaller storms. A donation to an environmental cause, a morning spent educating patients about vaccines. Recycling, buying less, showing up to vote. It all feels inadequate, way too small, but better than doing nothing. Better than pretending the storm will pass and leave us all unscathed.

TWELVE

Detach

I am on the phone with Devon, a twenty-seven-year-old woman who is my former patient. I took care of Devon from the time she was eighteen until the time I stopped practicing internal medicine a few years ago. She had an active eating disorder and was twenty pounds underweight when I first met her. Her skin was sallow and she had dark circles under big, blue, dark-lashed eyes. Her long blonde hair was dull and thinning.

She also struggled with a condition called fibromyalgia, in which the brain seems to amplify pain signals. Her whole body hurt. She had stiffness, fatigue, and sleep problems. Both eating disorders and fibromyalgia are associated with depression; despite antidepressant medications, Devon felt sad and despondent.

Working with me, a psychiatrist, and a physical therapist, Devon gained some weight and got better control over her pain through non-narcotic medications, physical therapy, and psychotherapy. Her depression waxed and waned, but she began to feel hopeful much of the time. She was doing well when I left practice, and I turned her care over to a nurse practitioner who understood her problems.

Now, several years later, Devon still has my phone number and has texted me, hoping we can talk.

"Thank you for calling me back," she tells me softly. "The nurse practitioner you referred me to was great. But she moved to New York last year."

Uh oh, I think. I know there aren't a lot of people around who are comfortable working with eating disorder patients or those with chronic pain. But Devon tells me her situation now is worse than just lacking a primary care practitioner or internist. Recently, Devon's psychiatrist stopped accepting her insurance. She's been on a search for new medical care since then. So far, she can't locate any psychiatrists who both take her insurance and have time for a new patient. COVID has made that worse; with the stress of the pandemic, there are now long waitlists for mental healthcare. She's also seen two different primary care doctors, but both deemed not only her depression but also her pain to be psychiatric problems. They won't adjust her medications, even though her fibromyalgia has flared up, and they have no other suggestions.

I give her a couple of referrals—one to a rheumatologist I think can help with the pain, and another to a mental health clinic near her. Mostly I listen. She has developed a lot more resilience than when I first met her, but her current situation is testing that. Some tweaks to her medications might help, but much of what she needs is understanding and support, maybe some encouragement to improve her nutrition and get some gentle exercise. Support to persevere through a difficult time, and a reminder that things will get better. That she has more strength than she recognizes right now. I know this about her because I've seen her rally before.

I feel a twinge of guilt because I'm not available to Devon as a doctor anymore. I can't adjust her medications or prescribe a new course of physical therapy. I don't have an office or the right malpractice insurance to provide that kind of ongoing care.

I'm a tipping boat, tipping over toward my wish to fix everything for everyone. Tipping toward what broke me. We all need support, and I didn't have the help I needed to do this work—intensive, time-intensive, heart-intensive care for my patients. I've put my own pieces back together, but I can't do it for others anymore. I quickly right myself.

"Devon, let's talk again in a couple of weeks," I say. "Hopefully by then, you'll have an appointment to see this new rheumatologist. I'm here to listen and support you for now."

I hang up the phone, feeling sad and frustrated that she's being treated as though her body and her head are separate, told that she must have a psychiatrist fix her head, and that a medical doctor can only try to fix her body. Most likely, the psychiatrist and the internist or rheumatologist will never even speak to each other given the pace of care these days. No one involved in her care seems to see that her head and body are attached.

My musings about detached heads brings to mind the Barbie dolls I so loved when I was a child. The heads of those dolls were easily removed from their bodies back then, though I've heard the newer editions have a more secure attachment. My brother and his friends enjoyed beheading Barbie dolls, which horrified me when I was very young, when dressing my beautiful silky-haired Barbies in their tiny matching outfits was an important activity for me. They represented the untarnished, uncomplicated yet glamorous life I might build for myself. Barbies, in the '70s could become anything—executives, models, athletes, doctors, actresses, princesses. They had equally well-dressed boyfriends, as well as cars, homes, and even castles. Barbies had beautiful friends and lovely cousins and adorable little sisters. They were supposed to be teenagers but had no homework and no parents anywhere in sight to tell them what to do.

Once I hit a certain age, maybe twelve, Barbie dolls lost their appeal. I began to think about the unrealistic bodies they inhabited—smooth, hairless, nipple-less, and sex-organless with tiny waists and perfect, high breasts. I was an anatomically correct, imperfect pre-teen, and I would never look like Barbie. My life was also a real life, with parents, homework, chores and typical kid problems, like mean girls at school and fights with my brother, something Barbie would never endure.

I started removing the heads from my own Barbies, then. Once a head was removed, you could stick it back on the neck, but the attachment was never stable again. Once apart, the body and head were always at risk of becoming separated again.

Devon, despite her long blonde hair and blue eyes, is not a Barbie doll. She's a real-life person, with real-life feelings and concerns and an anatomically correct body that does not have a detachable head. Yet she's being asked to separate her mind from her body.

"Take this Gabapentin for the nerves in your body, to shut off the pain," I imagine Doctor #1 saying to her. "Then go to Doctor #2, and he'll tell you what to do about your head. I only take care of bodies."

I don't believe that happened, not exactly. Nor do I believe the primary care doctors she went to really believe that the mind and body are separate entities. I think the truth is more likely that the doctors she saw either weren't quite sure how to integrate the physical and emotional in Devon's care, or they simply didn't have the time and energy.

We weren't taught much in medical school about integration of mind and body. Our lectures taught us anatomy, microbiology, pathology, physiology, and pathophysiology. We learned the normal and the abnormal, we learned the organ systems. Case studies during small group learning might encourage students to think through the emotional component of physical illness, or the physical manifestations of a psychiatric problem, but it's not nearly enough. Clinical rotations involve one or two months at a time in different specialties and subspecialties, often in the hospital with seriously ill patients. This approach, if anything, further separates one discipline from another, rather than integrating mind and body. A rare mentor might include a student in thinking through a mind-body patient problem, but it's not the norm.

In residency, there's not much time for the kind of thinking that goes into cases like Devon's. The focus is on efficiency and prioritizing the management of life-threatening issues over those that only threaten the quality of life. While lip-service might be given to "treating the whole person," we learned tacitly that it was not a good idea to explore the patients' emotions too thoroughly. The hidden curriculum, learned from watching and imitating many of our superiors, taught us that digging too deeply into a patient's story was like opening Pandora's box, and that it would be stressful and time-consuming, if not impossible, to stuff everything back in and close the lid.

We also weren't encouraged to explore our own emotions as they related to our care of patients. Who had time to dwell on their own feelings when there were sick patients waiting to be seen in clinic, or to be admitted to the hospital, or to be diagnosed and treated and sent home so new patients could occupy their beds? Even if we wanted to examine our own inner lives, there was no safe place to do it within our training programs. Feelings weren't a common topic between residents. There was always too much to accomplish, and perhaps we were afraid of what we'd find out if we opened up to one another. Meetings with attendings were strictly for patient management.

I did have one attending ask me about feelings, but not in a helpful way. As a medical intern, I spent a month caring for patients on the inpatient oncology service.

The attending oncologist, a middle-aged woman with long, frizzy hair dyed pitch-black and frighteningly pale skin, reminded me of Morticia Addams. She wore hippie dresses and purple suede boots with fringe and spoke in a low, throaty tone. Many of the patients on our service had end-stage cancer, and it seemed like half of them died in the hospital, the last place I would want to spend my final days. Sometimes it seemed like we were morticians rather than physicians.

Mr. Jones, an emaciated middle-aged man with metastatic

lung cancer, was admitted to our service for chemotherapy. The senior resident on the team questioned Morticia's decision to administer chemo to a man so frail, but Morticia felt we should forge ahead, and Mr. Jones consented. He wasn't ready to give up, but he'd see how things progressed.

Late the next evening, during an overnight shift in the hospital, I was called to evaluate Mr. Jones, whose blood pressure had dropped. Arriving on the oncology floor at about midnight, I was met with the odor of feces, mixed with the distinct metallic scent of blood. Mr. Jones had begun bleeding briskly from his gastrointestinal tract and was semi-conscious.

Despite transfusions and IV fluids running wide open into his veins, Mr. Jones' condition continued to deteriorate. I called Morticia, who suggested we obtain a radiology test called a bleeding scan to localize the site of the G.I. bleed.

"Can we call Mr. Jones' family and ask them for a Do Not Resuscitate (DNR) order?" I asked. "I don't think he's going to make it. I don't want him to die with us pounding on his chest."

"I'll call you back about that," Morticia said. "Go ahead with the scan for now."

In the radiology suite, as the radiologist began the test, Mr. Jones continued to bleed. I stood outside the room, helpless, watching through a window as he lay unconscious on a cold metal table. Then his heart stopped, and a code blue was called. We didn't have the DNR order, so we went ahead with CPR. Mr. Jones died in a sterile room with strangers pumping his chest, breaking his fragile ribs, instead of with his family holding his hand.

After the failed resuscitation attempt, I sat alone outside the radiology suite, shivering in surgical scrubs soiled with blood and feces. It was just after 7 a.m. I'd been awake for more than twenty-four hours and had a whole day of work ahead of me. I was already late for work rounds with the rest of my team.

Arriving on the oncology unit, still in dirty scrubs, Morticia asked me to recount the events leading to Mr. Jones' death. I took a deep breath, but when I spoke my voice quivered. Tears streamed down my cheeks as I recalled the blood, the cold radiology suite, my patient's final moments.

Later, Morticia would ask me to meet her in her office.

"I'm concerned that you're having a problem dealing with death," she told me when I arrived there.

"Not death *per se*. But the kind of death Mr. Jones had? Yes, I have a problem with that. And with life. My life. I'd been up all night watching Mr. Jones bleed out. I was covered in blood and stool, and I had a whole day of patient care ahead of me. Am I really supposed to be okay with all that?"

"Well, you have to be."

"I'm fine now," I lied. In fact, I was traumatized. I'd felt powerless, because I was outside the room, watching through a window, unable to help my patient. I had a sense of guilt, a feeling that there was something more I could have done, but I didn't know what it was. I was angry at Morticia because she hadn't called back, hadn't given any indication whether she'd asked for a DNR order or even spoken to the family. I also had existential dread, realizing this sort of bleak end could happen to anyone, including me. But Morticia didn't feel like a safe person with whom to process these feelings.

"Well, good," she replied. "You have to detach."

Does one have to detach in order to care for sick patients? It seems clear that, in the moment, at the time of an emergency, some distance is essential. Putting emotion aside to think clearly and logically is a necessity. Thinking critically in a medical emergency means rapidly running algorithms and scenarios through the mind: What is happening to this person? What's the most likely cause? What are the options for management? What are the steps I need to take?

What doesn't make sense to me is to push feelings aside permanently, to sweep them away as though they don't exist. In fact, I don't think it's even possible. I used to believe it was. I would just keep moving, working, getting things done after emotional or stressful events, proud of myself for my professionalism and my ability to prioritize. I'd tell myself that I'd deal with it later or think I was magically processing the events beneath the surface, but I wouldn't ever take the time to actually sit with the feelings.

When I was in the third year of medical school, my father developed chest pain and had a triple bypass surgery in California, where my parents lived at the time. I needed to fly to San Diego to see him and keep my mother company during and right after the surgery. I was more than halfway through my internal medicine rotation. To get credit, I could only take three or four days off, or I'd have to start all over. My father's surgery went well, but he was still in Surgical Intensive Care when I returned to Philly. I was worried about him, and I also felt I was abandoning my mother when she still needed company. Nevertheless, I returned and threw myself back into my clinical rotation. I thought I was fine.

It was only after my dad was home and on the mend that the feelings of fear and loss I'd stuffed away came back to bite me. As I headed into yet another new clinical rotation, this time in radiology. I began to have trouble concentrating. I felt jumpy and nervous. I tried cutting back my coffee intake, but then I felt jumpy, nervous, and exhausted. Fortunately, it was a month with very little patient care. We observed some radiologic procedures, but mostly we attended lectures and practiced reading x-rays. My concentration difficulties significantly affected my ability to process the information, and I learned less than I would have hoped, but passed the course.

Eventually the symptoms improved, but it brought back the memory of other episodes of anxiety I'd had in college and even high school. It wasn't until much later, in psychotherapy, that I understood the relationship between my anxiety and feelings I'd refused to let myself experience.

Knowing the potential cost of distancing myself from emotions wasn't enough to prevent me from doing it ever again. When my mother died in 1990, I was already overwhelmed after starting my first job as an attending doctor and having my first child only months earlier. My initial reaction of grief and anguish was quickly supplanted by the need to help my father make funeral arrangements, to comfort others around me, and to continue caring for my infant.

Back at work only a week later, I was afraid to allow myself to think or feel for fear I would not be able to keep up my breakneck pace. It didn't occur to me to take time off, and nobody around me suggested it. But deep feelings have a way of emerging, and a long period of ill health and low-grade depression followed.

In his 2014 book *The Body Keeps the Score*, psychiatrist Bessel Van Der Kolk describes how the brain and the body are both affected by traumatic events. Through changes in neurochemicals and hormones, physical changes and physical symptoms may accompany or even replace emotional symptoms after stressful occurrences. We may be able to behave as though nothing has happened, to detach from the cognitive part of our feelings, but our bodies know better.

If the suffering of patients is potentially traumatic for physicians, who do we serve by detaching from our feelings of sadness or fear? It surely doesn't serve the physician, at least not in the long run. Perhaps it is easier to feel nothing, to be numb, but our minds and bodies won't allow that to go on forever. We ourselves will eventually suffer, turning to substances or other addictions to help us remain numb, or developing physical or emotional symptoms if we don't face our demons directly. Our loved ones will likely be negatively affected by our troubles, so we are not serving our families or friends either.

Ongoing detachment from our feelings also doesn't serve our patients. The gamut of emotions, both good and bad, is part of being human. While knowledge and technology and medications may help patients and even cure serious disease, the act of healing is more than prescribing drugs and performing procedures. Healing is a profoundly human phenomenon, and our presence as human beings facilitates it. Cut off from my own feelings, I have less compassion, less empathy, and less energy for my patients.

Perhaps detachment serves the institutions that train and employ physicians, as it keeps us moving. Residents, who are responsible for much of the day-to-day patient care in hospitals, don't miss a beat between a patient death and the next task on their to-do list. Physicians return to work just days after a family member dies, just a few weeks after a baby is born, hours after a minor trauma like a car accident, and refuse to go home when sick. Work ethic is maintained, the flow remains unbroken. But at what cost in the long run when detachment finally fails as a defense mechanism?

A physician who is detached from her own emotions wouldn't be a good match for a patient like Devon, one who has such intertwined emotional and physical symptoms. By the time I met Devon, I had gotten pretty good at feeling my feelings, at sitting with them and letting them happen. I was aware of my own sense of sadness around Devon, as I cared about her and saw her struggling. I knew I felt helpless to change her circumstances, and that sometimes I felt frustrated by her resistance to changing her behavior.

That self-awareness made it easier for me to sit with Devon in her sadness and pain without becoming overwhelmed. I could separate my feelings from the reality of my role as her doctor. I understood that feelings change and move and pass, and that allowing them to happen wasn't a bad thing. That in turn helped her to be less overwhelmed, and we could then work on treating what I could, like her muscle spasms and her vitamin D deficiency.

This sort of encounter, though, is time-consuming and takes emotional energy. I couldn't sit behind my computer screen and order her blood tests or her medications while we talked; she needed my full attention and presence. As an employed doctor, I was only granted fifteen to twenty minutes for a follow-up visit, which was wholly inadequate when considering all of Devon's needs. I stole time from other, less complicated visits, or only addressed one or two problems at a time and brought her back at short intervals. Eventually, the stress of trying to treat many such complicated patients without adequate time or support contributed to my burnout and unhappiness in my last few years of practice.

Hearing Devon tell me the doctors she had seen seemed dismissive and pushed her care off to someone else makes sense in today's medical environment. Doctors don't have the time to even gather all the necessary history for such a complex case in a single visit. They are already so overwhelmed with their workloads that the thought of caring for patients with chronic problems with no obvious solutions, patients whose treatment requires trial and error and creativity, seems untenable. I can't blame them. They're simply trying to save themselves from drowning. I didn't do that, and it took me out of the water entirely.

There is harm done, though, when a patient leaves a visit with the message that they can't be helped. Even when we need to refer to another professional (in this case, a psychiatrist), we can at very least ally with our patient. Even when we fear opening Pandora's box, we need to look at the suffering, acknowledge it, and stand with the patient.

When medical care is a business rather than a profession, and care is dictated by time demands and productivity rather than by individual needs, when doctors have to choose between saving ourselves or giving our all to our patients, it is no longer a safe space for anyone. When we detach heads from bodies, intellect from emotion, and treating from healing, we deny the humanity of everyone involved.

How then do we re-integrate, and re-attach? Is medicine like an old, decapitated Barbie, the head now forever separate? Perhaps we need a new model. A new edition. One with a more secure attachment.

THIRTEEN

Grow Old Along with Me

Grow old along with me
The best is yet to be
When our time has come
We will be as one

—*Robert Browning*

It's 6:45 p.m., and I pace in front of the bedroom window, gazing down the street every couple of minutes. Here comes Larry, finally, around the curve of the road, bike pedals slowing as he turns and coasts up the driveway. I exhale, and head down the stairs.

He meets me in the kitchen.

"Hi! How's your day been?" he asks. Casual, carefree. The cleats from his bike shoes click on the stone tile floor. Clad in spandex from neck to knees, a colorful bike jersey, one of the many in his collection, over a unitard he calls "bib shorts," he stands near the counter, dripping with sweat. The LED headlamp attached to his helmet remains on, glaring directly into my eyes. I clench my teeth.

"Good," I reply. "How was yours?"

Our evening will proceed. Larry will shower and change, and we will make dinner together, standing at the granite counter, Larry chopping vegetables for our stir-fry while I sauté garlic and sear chicken. Our little mixed-breed rescue dog will beg for tastes of human food.

Larry and I will chat about our respective days. We won't talk about my pacing or my clenched teeth. I have taken a vow of silence regarding his bicycle commuting.

Larry started biking to work in 2006. He'd been complaining for years about how stressful it was to drive to work each day, fighting what constantly seemed like rush hour traffic, even though, as a hospital-based physician, he left the house by 7 a.m. and often didn't return until after 6 p.m. After seeing Al Gore's documentary, *An Inconvenient Truth*, Larry told me, "That's it. I'm not driving to work anymore. I'll bike commute every day. I'll do my part for the environment and get my exercise that way." Larry is a man of great resolve. He doesn't make such declarations lightly.

Never mind that for more than half the year, he is either coming or going in the dark.

Never mind that his commute takes him on busy streets and through part of North Philadelphia known as the "badlands" because of drug and gang-related crime. Belmont Plateau, an area he rides through daily, is known as a place where drug dealers peddle their wares, and there are nearly daily shootings in the blocks around Temple Hospital and Medical School where Larry works. Still, the only thing that stops him from riding his bike to work is heavy snow or ice.

Our friends tell him he is going to get hit by a car and die. Our friend Mark, who stopped riding a bike in the city years ago after seeing a cyclist get hit by a car, asks every time we see him if Larry has given up bike commuting yet.

"No. I love my bike commute," Larry replies serenely.

"Seriously, Larry," Mark replies, "you should think again. It's not a matter of 'if' you get hit, but 'when.'"

"I've been riding for years, and I'm fine. I'm not going to get hit," says Larry with authority.

It doesn't matter that one of my medical school professors died in such an accident twenty years ago, or that, more recently, a friend who was inspired by Larry's determination to start riding his bike to work was hit by an SUV and had to be airlifted to a trauma center on his very first bicycle commute.

There have been near misses: the truck that blew through a stop sign just when Larry was crossing the off-ramp to the expressway (Larry saw it coming and leaped off his bike, which was mangled, though he escaped with just bruises) and a tire caught in trolley track (Larry will tell you his broken scapula was a minor problem and that, again, the bike fared worse than he did).

He often comes home with cuts and scrapes from "little falls."

Always pragmatic, Larry cites studies: "According to the CDC, the odds of dying in a car accident far outweigh the odds of dying in a bicycle accident," he informs me.

If one looks strictly at risk data, this, in fact, is true. The "lifetime odds" of dying in a car crash in the U.S. are one in three hundred and three. The "lifetime odds" of dying in a cycling accident in the us are one in 4,717. But I refute this data. It looks like cycling is far safer than driving, but to compare these odds makes the assumption that as many people ride bicycles as drive cars. It also does not take into account that many cycling trips occur on trails without cars or on quiet streets, while Larry's cycle commuting takes him on major roads, greatly increasing the chance of a serious accident. In truth, we can't calculate his specific risks. Our positions are heavily weighted with emotion. Larry believes his safety equipment and the light-reflecting strips on his spandex, along with his superior skills as a bicycle commuter, will prevent a serious accident. And perhaps he's right. Helmets and lights and vigilance reduce risk. Experience means he's less likely to make a dangerous error in judgment. Still, I can't stop worrying.

Six or seven years ago, after he fell off his bicycle and walked into the house with bloody abrasions over both knees, he told me he'd go back to driving if I adamantly opposed bike commuting. He sat on the edge of the white tub in our master bath while I dabbed at his wounds with a wet washcloth, trying to remove the last bits of gravel from his torn skin.

"I hate that it upsets you," he said, "but I hope you can live with it, because it makes me happy."

How could I veto an activity that brings my husband joy?

Instead, we struck a bargain. He would wear a cyclist's bracelet with his name and emergency contact information engraved in it. He would text me when he gets to work, and again when he's about to leave work to head home. If something happens to him, I will know. He won't be left, broken and bleeding, his bicycle frame mangled, on the side of a road. In return, I promised to refrain from constantly reminding him of the risk he is taking, or of my anxiety about said risk.

This "compromise" is tenuous. Neither of us is completely satisfied. He finds himself having to "check in" like an errant teenager. I am full of silent reproach, ever the disapproving parent. I channel the histrionic home-bound woman, flinging herself at the cool, detached lover leaving for an adventure. We rehearse and perfect our parts, the unwilling actors in a play about stereotypical gender roles.

My fear is an embarrassment, my caution a proof of failure at my own quest, because, in my own life, I believe myself to be bold and irrepressible. I'm not a delicate flower; I can pitch a tent and build a fire, and I've had my share of scrapes and bruises from the great outdoors. I'm also no stranger to inner city strife. I've lived and worked in all manner of urban neighborhoods.

In my years as a physician, I've encountered guns in the E.R., switchblades in medical clinics, and plenty of patients who were angry or just plain belligerent.

I feel burned by the anxiety I have now; an ounce of denial would be a soothing salve. I've tried to develop denial, grow it like cells in a culture medium, exercise it as a muscle I can strengthen, but my cells refuse to divide. The muscle remains flaccid.

I remind myself all risk is relative. To live is to take the risk of dying over and over each day. We each make judgments about the risk and benefit of every activity we undertake. We make constant, specific, but usually unspoken, declarations about which actions are worth the risk posed by them. We make general, also usually unspoken, declarations about the amount of risk we each will tolerate. I will hike in the wilderness, ski downhill on the black diamonds, raft on whitewater. I love the periodic adrenaline rush of slightly risky physical activity, which makes my objection to Larry's cycling seem all the more irrational. I am inconsistent and contradictory. Perhaps these activities feel safer because we usually ski and hike and raft together or in groups, while Larry's cycle-commuting is done alone. I have no way to know if he is safe, so my imagination is free to roam, unchecked, through the possible accidents he could have. Beyond that, I think it's the daily repetition that wears me down.

Our friend Bruce, a recreational thrill-seeker, argues that the more risk we take, the more alive we actually are. I won't go that far. I don't want to be dropped out of an airplane or to try and climb Everest (two activities Bruce aspires to), but I also don't want fear to dictate everything I do.

Larry and I have been married thirty years. I don't think of us as old, not yet. Larry has just passed sixty; I am heading directly toward it. We are still energetic and active, though the early signs of decrepitude are creeping up on us—aches and pains, the need for ibuprofen a couple of times a week. Actuarial tables estimate that Larry will live another twenty-two years, and I will live another twenty-seven. Studies on happiness and aging say that, on average, Americans are happiest with their lives in the second half of their seventies. The best part of our lives is, perhaps, yet to come. That is, unless an unexpected cause of early death strikes one of us.

Larry says he doesn't often think about the potential for premature death. He makes the assumption, over and over, that it won't happen. I, on the other hand, touch base with my fear of it at least a few times a day. The cycling. A car accident, especially in inclement weather.

Sudden onset of illness. Sudden cardiac death, though neither of us is at increased risk for it. One or both of us could be struck down by any of these scenarios at any time. I don't dwell on that or worry about it at length; the knowledge of it just lurks on the edge of my consciousness.

We are both physicians, similarly trained, but even that seems to have affected us differently in this regard. Bodies, human bodies, are magnificent and miraculous in all that they can do. They are amazingly resilient, fending off invading pathogens, healing in the face of horrific damage. Larry always thinks about the resilience, clings to it.

"Most of the illnesses we see are self-limiting," he declares, when we talk about our work. True enough.

But bodies are also just a conglomeration of cells, and the cells can wear down or wear out or go awry. They can destroy and be destroyed. This is what I see, and I watch for signs that we are at the beginning of some sort of destruction.

Is one way of being "better" than the other? Is one of us "right" and the other "wrong"? Sometimes it seems that having more denial would allow me to live more serenely in the world, to suffer less, especially since so many risks are either unavoidable or so subjective in their magnitude that I can't judge if my trepidation is reasonable. But how much denial is optimal? When does it become dangerous—a flirtation with peril? Neuroscience tells us fear is hardwired in the limbic system, an ancient part of the brain, and that the fear response is not only normal, but necessary to protect oneself from danger. When is it a good thing for denial to tamp down fear, and when does it become a liability? The answer is obvious if I am being attacked by a tiger and equally obvious if I am being attacked by a gnat. But what about the gray zone in between? Isn't most of life somewhere in between?

What happened on Thanksgiving five years ago was an instance of dangerous denial.

Larry fell ill with a fever and malaise the Monday before Thanksgiving. He powered through his workday, a tactic familiar to most doctors, as we tend to be workaholics and to feel we must put our patients first, even when we're sick. On Tuesday, he went to work but left early after spiking a high temperature and developing shaking chills. I came home to find him sitting in the overstuffed chair in the corner of our bedroom, wrapped in a blanket and popping TUMS.

"What's going on?" I ask. "You said you felt okay when you left for work this morning."

"I have the flu," he replies. "I'll be fine."

"Your office mates said you had shaking chills," I inform him. "And what's with the TUMS? Is your stomach upset?"

"Why are my colleagues calling you?" Larry asks, peeved.

"They're your friends. *Our* friends. And they were worried about you, so they called me."

"I'm FINE. I just need to be left alone. I took ibuprofen. I guess I took too much ibuprofen, because my stomach is a little upset from it, but I'm FINE. I just want to sleep," he pleads.

Destruction, I think. *This is not ordinary. This is not the flu.* My intuition is working. Maybe it's working overtime. I say nothing. Messing with Larry when he's talking in capital letters means war.

He looks even worse the next day. At least he stays home from work.

"I think you should see a doctor," I tell him.

"I *am* a doctor." He is sitting in the chair again, shivering in a blanket. "I know it's the flu. What is a doctor going to do for me? It would be a poor use of medical resources to go to a doctor."

"You can't diagnose yourself. You shouldn't be your own doctor. And tomorrow is Thanksgiving, so if there's really something wrong, you'll end up in the E.R."

"I'll be FINE by tomorrow. I'm getting better." His tone is dangerous.

"You don't look better." *Destruction*.

He ignores me and waves me away. He sleeps and drinks fluids and takes ibuprofen. I try to believe him. I try not to believe my mounting worry.

That night, he soaks the sheets in sweat.

Drenching night sweats are a bad sign, says the undefended voice in my head.

"See, my fever is breaking," says my husband.

Thanksgiving morning, his skin looks a bit gray, but he says he feels much better. He says he is FINE. We go to his sister's house, just a mile away, for Thanksgiving. Their parents and another sibling and all of our young adult children are there. Larry sleeps in the den most of the day.

"What's wrong with Larry? He looks terrible," says his father, Al, a retired family doctor. He is sitting in an armchair in my sister-in-law's living room, wearing his retirement uniform of stiff blue jeans and a plaid flannel shirt. His glasses are slightly askew as he ruffles through a newspaper.

"I don't know. He says it's the end of the flu, and he won't get care. I'm concerned," I say, hoping for some help.

Al just shrugs.

"I'm sure he'll be fine," he says.

I forgot that he is the original King of Denial.

At dinner, the long table is overflowing with platters of turkey and brisket, bowls of mashed potatoes and cranberry sauce, tureens of roasted vegetables, gravy boats and ladles. Larry only eats a pecan. Just one pecan. Nobody else seems to notice. Everyone is talking at once at the table, passing plates of food, sipping wine, thinking about the pies and the chocolate peanut butter cake lining the kitchen counters, waiting for their turn.

The pecan is my call to action. I am done with the charade. As the kids clear the table and the adults head for the living room, I rummage in my sister-in-law's medicine cabinet for a thermometer and ambush Larry in the hall. His temperature is 103.5.

"It's time to go to the E.R.," I tell him. "You are sick. If you don't get in the car and go, I'm going to divorce you. This is the most foolish behavior I've ever seen from you. Either you go, or I'm going to leave here without you, and tell the kids not to bring you home. Your family of origin can deal with your bullshit. And you know how they'll deal with it? They'll ignore you, and you'll die on the floor, and they'll just step right over you."

"Okay, okay. Fine. But my dad wants a family picture, so let's do that first."

"Are you serious? We have to do a family picture when you have a 103.5 temperature?"

"Yes."

"Fuck. You are crazy."

We leave the bathroom to find the family lining up for the yearly Thanksgiving photo.

"Oh, there you are," says Larry's dad. "Roz, get in back. Larry, sit down in front with the guys."

The King of Denial snaps the picture. I see Larry wincing as he rises. *He's got an acute abdomen. He's going to need surgery*, the undefended voice in my head tells me. I make excuses to his family, tell my kids half the truth, and push him out the door.

"This is a very poor use of medical resources," Larry tells me, as I half carry him to the car for the ten-minute trip to the E.R.

"Yes, you said something about that yesterday. If you wanted to make better use of resources, you would have seen a doctor days ago," I reply in as neutral a tone as I can muster.

At the E.R., he is sent immediately to CT scan. He has diverticulitis, an illness that is often mild and managed with antibiotics.

But Larry's diverticulitis is much more severe; his colon has ruptured, and he has peritonitis. In fact, the rupture likely occurred three days ago, when he had shaking chills.

Because of his otherwise excellent health, he escapes immediate surgery, which would have included a temporary colostomy, and is admitted for intravenous fluids and antibiotics. The first forty-eight hours are touch-and-go, the surgeon ready to intervene at any moment if Larry doesn't rally. He spends this time in a unit just one step down from Intensive Care, attached to a heart monitor, in and out of a morphine-laced sleep.

As I wandered the hushed hallways in the hospital during those initial two days, I reviewed the events of Larry's illness in my mind. Why hadn't I been more assertive? Why hadn't I pushed harder? Had it been because I'd doubted my own perceptions?

I would not have done this with a patient; in my clinic I am dispassionate, clear-headed. I know who is sick, and who is not. I triage and treat, convey caution to the cavalier, calm the fears of the overanxious. Nor would I have doubted myself with my children, for whom my intuition is so well-honed that it approaches prescience. But my husband's confidence was such that I lost my own. His denial dictated our actions, to his detriment. Now he might end up with a colostomy. Now, he could die.

I'll kill you if you die, I thought. I was angry at him for lying in a bed, floating on morphine, leaving me to handle this alone. I was angry at myself for listening to him when he said he was FINE, but I knew he wasn't. I was just angry. W*e're supposed to grow old together*.

I'm going to listen to you in the future," Larry told me, once he recovered.

"Maybe it's not listening to me," I replied. "Maybe it's just paying attention to what your body is telling you. Maybe it's not trying to be such a hero all the time."

"You're right," he ceded quietly.

In the past, I would have been thrilled to hear that I was right. But now that "rightness" is a hollow victory. I didn't want to be right. I didn't want Larry to be wrong. I wanted to believe we could make the right decisions to keep ourselves alive.

Before 1990, I might have acted just like Larry had in the first days of his illness. I turned thirty in 1990. I had my first child in 1990. Neither of those events would have, alone, changed my mindset, but other things happened that did.

In my young life, before age thirty, I had already been through a series of medical issues: meningitis at age four, an episode of arthritis possibly portending an autoimmune disease at age sixteen, a hospitalization for an eye infection that threatened my cornea at age twenty, a yearlong bout of colitis in my mid-twenties, and chronic migraines (shared with my mother) since age ten.

My father became extremely protective of my health from the time of the meningitis, keeping me home from school for sniffles and whipping out a bottle of a bitter elixir called terpin hydrate if I coughed even once, trying to talk me out of any activity that might result in injury. I know I caused him endless worry. But I was young and reckless, and the more he fussed over me, the more determined I was not to be sick.

I bucked against any kind of physical limitations. I ignored warnings and believed I was invincible. I proved my invincibility to myself by skiing and skating, hiking in the wilderness, and experimenting with pot and alcohol as a teen. I thought I'd proved it to everyone else by getting through medical school and a rigorous residency during which sleep deprivation and forty-hour work shifts were the norm.

By the end of residency, I was not only still alive, but, inexplicably, I was well, save an occasional migraine. And I was a doctor, married and pregnant with my first child. Denial had apparently worked in my favor.

Max was born in September of 1990. My pregnancy had been smooth and easy. I thought I had life under control. But Max turned blue in the newborn nursery and was transferred to Newborn Intensive Care. Unable to find a cause, the neonatologists sent him home on an apnea monitor. It could happen again, they said. It could be related to sudden infant death syndrome.

Deeply shaken, I tried to return to "normal" life, but suddenly the world was not a safe place.

The apnea monitor alarm went off now and then, and we would run, panicked, to Max's crib. Each time, we found him not just breathing, but pink, awake, and moving.

After a few months, the pediatrician took the monitor away.

"I knew there was nothing wrong with him," Larry told me.

I knew no such thing. I didn't reply.

We'd been without the apnea monitor just a few weeks when my mother died suddenly at the age of sixty-two. She'd most likely had a massive stroke. But there'd been no indication she was ill. Now, I was certain that was terrifying and capricious.

Soon after my mother's death, I had some routine blood tests, and my liver function tests were abnormal. A workup revealed I had chronic hepatitis C, a bloodborne viral disease I almost certainly contracted as a health-care worker in a high-risk urban hospital. I had no symptoms, and there was no immediate threat. The problem with hep C is that, over a period of years, it causes progressive liver damage, and can lead to liver failure or cancer in some (but not all) patients. Because research around hep C was in its infancy at that time, early in the 1990s, the only treatment available was an experimental protocol known to have unpleasant side effects. The chance of cure with it was only twenty-five percent. My prognosis without treatment was a complete unknown, and it wasn't much better with treatment. Any remaining denial of life's cruel randomness was pried loose from me by this information.

I felt abandoned and lost when Larry continued to court optimism.

"You're going to be fine," he told me as he sat in a vinyl chair next to the hospital bed where I waited for the doctor to perform my first liver biopsy. "We'll get through this, and you'll get treated."

We were in a gloomy old wing of the Hospital of the University of Pennsylvania. The pale green walls were scuffed and the cracks in the paint made me think of veins, which led my mind right back to my liver.

"No, *I'll* get through this," I retorted bitterly. "And we don't know if I'm going to be fine. The treatment is toxic and has very little chance of working."

"If it doesn't work, there will be something else."

"If I don't die first."

In retrospect, it's a good thing one of us still had some denial. We had a child. We had careers. We had a life together. There was no option but to keep moving forward and to fight. I'm not sure I could have done that without Larry's belief in a good outcome. But that didn't keep me from resenting it. It didn't seem fair that he could still go through life with equanimity when I couldn't. It was only much later that I realized how hard he worked to push back his fear so there would be room for mine.

As it turned out, he was right, at least in the long term. I completed two unsuccessful trials of experimental medication before an improved protocol, with a slightly higher response rate, cured me in 1998. Ultimately, Larry's assessment that, even if there was no answer for hepatitis C twenty years ago, there eventually would be one, has even come to pass, as drugs with cure rates close to ninety-eight percent became available by 2014.

Despite the good fortune of my cure, I wasn't able to recover my capacity for denial. The universe continued to seem chaotic and random. I also developed an impatience for pragmatism. Data, useful for taking care of patients, no longer applied to my own life. After all, Max's breathing problem and my mother's death remained largely unexplained. My mother's risk of sudden death as a seemingly healthy sixty-two-year-old had been remote if you looked at statistics. My risk of hepatitis C was probably less than two percent. On the flip side, the experimental protocol should not have cured my hepatitis, either, yet I was cured. What was I to make of all this?

Without the comfort of evidence or the bliss of denial, I had no framework to rely on. I'd never believed in a personal God, so I didn't have prayer. I sometimes resorted to magical thinking: *We've been through a string of negative events. We're due for a period of peace*. Other times, I had to rely on my intuition, but I wasn't sure I could trust it. At some moments, I just assumed the worst and hoped for the best, an unhappily skewed form of fatalism I manufactured to prevent false hope. I think the distress this engendered in me led Larry to try to protect me when there were things I might not need to know.

The first time he kept medical information from me, it was about Max. By the time he left for college, our curly-haired, blue-eyed son had become a serious student-athlete. Though prone to sarcastic jokes and witty wordplay, he was a pretty level-headed young man. In his sophomore year at Wesleyan University, Max sustained a significant concussion during a wrestling match. He called home after the trainer had taken him for a neurologic evaluation and a CT scan of his head. Only Larry was home, and he suggested to Max that they keep this information to themselves. I imagine Larry didn't want to worry me. Max might have been afraid I'd push him to stop wrestling as I'd always been concerned about the risk of head injuries.

Fortunately, or unfortunately, he was due to come home for Thanksgiving less than a week after the head injury occurred. He arrived the Wednesday afternoon before Thanksgiving, while I was still at work.

When I got home, Max came to the front door to greet me. Larry was already home, standing in the hall behind him.

"Hi, Mom," Max said, leaning in for a hug. But I'd already seen his face, and something wasn't right. His eyes were bloodshot. He had a dazed, glazed-over look. I grabbed his shoulders and held him away from me to peer at him.

"Max, what's wrong with you? Are you drunk?" I asked him, alarmed. I saw Larry tense.

"Dad," Max said to Larry, "I guess we have to tell her."

Fortunately Max's brain healed over a short period of time. He returned to school after Thanksgiving weekend and to wrestling a few weeks later. Eventually, after another injury, he made his own decision to quit the sport.

I was furious at Larry for keeping the concussion a secret and laid into him.

"He's my son as well as yours. What gives you the right to play God? And what made you think I couldn't handle it? I've never given you any indication, in all these years of parenting, that I would be irrational or alarmist about injuries. All through high school, I've handled both kids' medical care, taken them to the doctor, to tests, to the E.R., sometimes without you when you weren't around."

"But I thought . . ." Larry began, but I interrupted before he could finish his sentence.

"Never do this again. What if there'd been complications to this concussion, and you'd never told me it happened in the first place?"

I was hard on him. Especially since I knew, even then, that he'd meant well. I hadn't needed protection; a concussion seemed pretty routine to me. But Larry had seen me at my worst moments. He wasn't sure what to expect. Besides, he had grown up with the King of Denial as a role model.

When Larry's mother was in her early forties, she developed thyroid cancer. His father conspired with her doctor, his colleague, to tell her only what she needed to know: that she had a lump on her thyroid, and it needed to be removed. The word cancer was never spoken. Later, he told Larry and their other three children that the "lump" was malignant, as they needed this information to manage their own medical care, but he swore them all to secrecy. Larry's mother is now eighty-eight-years-old, and she still has no idea she had cancer.

This kind of medical paternalism was common forty-five years ago, but is no longer considered acceptable. I don't know how Larry's mom would have reacted to a cancer diagnosis, but I think she had the right to know. I suspect she would have handled it with spirit. She's never been the fragile type. In all the time I've known her, she's been as tough as an unmarinated flank steak.

Larry apologized for trying to cover up Max's head injury, but he might have done it over again, given my unpredictable reactions to bad news. Even twenty years out from 1990, the worst year of my life, my coping was precarious. When our daughter was diagnosed with celiac disease as a teenager, I handled it with competency and grace, making sure she had the right foods and enough instruction on avoiding wheat to manage herself when she moved away for school. The same year, however, I fell apart after I had a minor car accident, weeping on and off for days and afraid to drive until my sister-in-law insisted I get behind the wheel and drive her around the block. One of our kids calling from college with a romantic problem might keep me up all night, but I took it in stride when Larry tore the cartilage in his knee and needed surgery.

I couldn't explain it then, but now I see it clearly. If a problem, even a big problem, had a solution, I was fine. I took charge. I did what needed to be done. What knocked me down was uncertainty and lack of control. My failure to recognize this and explain it to Larry contributed to our communication problems.

The most recent gaffe occurred only a few months ago. During a workup for some vague dizziness, Larry's ENT doctor ordered an MRI of his brain. I initially wasn't concerned. My own medical knowledge told me his symptoms were related to the inner ear, not the brain, and that his doctor was just covering all her bases. Larry had the same belief and scheduled the scan a week or so later. By then, his symptoms were long gone, but he followed through to be complete.

The morning of the MRI, though, I started to feel anxious. What if we were wrong, and this was the beginning of some sort of destruction? A malignant brain tumor or an aneurysm about to rupture?

"Call me with the results of your scan as soon as you have them, please?" I pleaded with Larry. I knew he could have results by 10 a.m. or noon at the latest, since he was having the MRI at the hospital where he'd worked for almost twenty years, and where he knew all the radiology staff and radiologists.

"I will, but it's going to be normal," he replied.

I was working at home, doing some medical editing. A little after noon, realizing I hadn't heard from Larry, I got up from my desk, went to the kitchen, and dialed his number.

"Hey, what's up?" he said, as though this were a normal day. It might have been, if we knew the scan was negative.

"Did you get the MRI results yet?" I asked, as I scooped some yogurt into a bowl. There was a beat of pause. One beat too many.

"No, it's not read yet."

"Are you sure? Maybe you should check with the neuro-radiologist." I wanted to believe him, but I felt like something wasn't right.

"If I don't hear by the end of the day, I'll call. I don't want to annoy anyone," he replied. Uneasy, I returned to my desk. I changed some wording in the paper I was reviewing, and looked up a citation to check accuracy. The document was about a disastrous blood disorder called aplastic anemia. *No wonder I worry, reading this kind of stuff,* I thought. I tried not to think about brain tumors. I tried to ignore the rising panic in my chest as the afternoon wore on.

At 4 p.m., I still hadn't heard from Larry and was about to call him again when I heard the kitchen door open. My heart began racing. Larry never comes home from work before six.

He popped his head into the study. He looked fine, despite his sweaty spandex bike outfit.

"I'm going to take a shower and change," he told me. He sounded normal. Too normal.

"Wait! Aren't you going to tell me about your MRI? I've been worried all day!"

He hesitated a moment. *Destruction.* I held my breath. Then he produced a small pile of papers from his bike pannier.

"Here's the report. I have a schwannoma on my ninth cranial nerve. It's very small. I'm waiting for a call back from someone from neurosurgery to find out what I have to do."

A schwannoma is a benign tumor made up of glial (Greek for glue) cells, which surround nerves to protect and bring nourishment to them. The ninth cranial nerve exits the brain at the base and innervates parts of the tongue and throat.

The medical knowledge Larry and I have in common was an immediate shortcut. I knew instantly he wasn't going to die from a brain tumor or an aneurysm. I knew this benign mass would not grow quickly or invade brain tissue, curling around the normal cells like the tendrils of an invasive vine. I knew it would not metastasize to distant organs. This schwannoma was not even responsible for Larry's dizziness.

I didn't know exactly what would need to happen next. Even a small, benign mass is not a good thing. Any space-occupying intracranial lesion is not a good thing. It could grow and press on adjacent nerves or on brain tissue. Any growth would need to be limited or stopped. In its current form, it might not need any treatment, and if it grew, there were options. Of course, I was concerned, but mostly I was relieved. Still, what I unleashed on my husband was anger.

"You knew this when I called you at noon, didn't you?" I asked, narrowing my eyes.

"Yes, but I didn't want to tell you over the phone. I was worried you'd be upset."

"I am upset. But not about the freaking schwannoma! I'm upset you lied to me. I'm upset you didn't trust me to handle this! I was terrified all day that you had a malignant brain tumor. And now I'm upset that you rode your bicycle home when you have a tumor in your head! You don't even know what you need to do yet. You haven't talked to your doctor, have you?"

I heard myself screeching. I knew I was being irrational.

Larry stood quietly waiting for me to finish. Instead, I burst into tears. Larry put his arms around me and let me cry into his spandex.

"I'm so sorry," Larry said. "I didn't realize you were worried all day. I thought it would be better not to tell you on the phone so you could look at the report and the papers I printed out on schwannomas. I was hoping I would have a definitive plan as to what to do before I told you, but that didn't happen."

"No, I'm sorry!" I sobbed. "I don't know why I'm yelling. I just knew all day that you were keeping something from me, and it scared me. You're a terrible liar! And you don't need to know the plan. I can help with that, help you set up appointments with the right people. But for now, I didn't even ask if you were okay!"

"I'm okay. I'm not upset about it. I'll do whatever I have to do about it. I did talk to my doctor, but she's an ENT, and this isn't even what caused my dizziness. This was just an incidental finding, and she doesn't know what to do about it. That's why I called one of the neurosurgeons. Of course we'll ultimately figure out the plan together."

I finally stopped crying. It was going to be fine. No destruction, at least not from the schwannoma, and not at that moment.

Later, I contemplated my reaction. Did I have any right to expect Larry to tell me his scan results as soon as he had gotten them? Wasn't it his right to decide when and how to tell me? Wasn't it his tumor? And yet, once another person is so inextricably bound up in your life, any problem, any crisis, belongs to both of you. The problem is no longer only about you, nor is the solution. I think he should have told me, but he didn't because he wasn't sure I'd react rationally. It gave him cause to infantilize and control me, like his father had done to his mother when she'd had thyroid cancer. This was exactly what I didn't want. I would have to be clear about what I could handle if I wanted him to share information.

A week later, we sat in an exam room at the radiation oncology department at the University of Pennsylvania with a neuro-radiation oncologist, Dr. C, reviewing Larry's scan. She pointed to a medium gray, dumbbell-shaped blob superimposed on several other shades of gray.

"So, there it is. It's very small. And you can see it's not pressing on any brain tissue or any of the other cranial nerves." We peered at the blob and the sea of slightly darker gray representing cerebrospinal fluid surrounding it.

"If this grows larger and starts to impinge on other structures, we can destroy it with a single dose of radiation—that's called Gamma Knife treatment. It's very precise. The risk of damaging the nerve is about one percent—very low. The risk of other side effects is even lower. But right now, I'd suggest we just monitor this. Get another scan in three months. If it hasn't grown, we can leave it alone."

I saw the crease in Larry's forehead relax, the edges of his mouth curl up.

"Dr. C, I just have one more question," Larry said. "Is there any reason I can't ride my bicycle with this schwannoma?" He was grinning at this point. Teasing me.

Of course, the answer was, "No."

"I still hate your bike commute," I tell Larry as he leaves for work in his spandex unitard and cleats. I haven't told him that part of what I hate is the spandex. It's not a great look on a man of a certain age.

"I know, and I'm sorry. I really don't want to give it up, though. I need it. I really am careful. I know it's not just about me," he replies. "I promise I'll quit if I start being klutzy as I get older."

"I don't like it, but I'm okay with it. It's not like you're skydiving every day. I want you to be happy. I believe you that you're careful."

I know now what I really hate is that I have no control over what happens. I can't make drivers want to share the road. I can't stop people from speeding or texting while they drive. But controlling my husband is not the answer.

I can't trust the world to be a safe or kind or fair place, but it's the only world we have. Ultimately, Larry and I want the same thing: we want to grow old together, and we also want to live our lives, to feel alive, for however long we are here.

———————— FOURTEEN ————————

More Magic, Less Misery

No health insurance? No, that's not a problem here. No, you won't get any bills from us. Your visit will be free. So will your medications and vaccines. You won't have to go to a pharmacy; our pharmacists will dispense your medication here.

You don't speak English? Don't worry, we have translators. No, not just Spanish. We'll call the language line if we don't have a translator who speaks your language.

Yes, I understand. You're worried that you might need expensive tests or visits to specialists. I see. You already know you need heart tests, but you couldn't get them because the hospital wanted you to pay up front. That's okay. We can give you an appointment with one of our cardiologists. If you need testing at the hospital, we can arrange it, free of charge to you.

Just so you know, we also have mental healthcare here. And we have eye care and dental care. We're happy you're here. Let's get started.

Are you wondering what planet you're on? Or at least thinking this medical facility is in a foreign country? Sounds like science fiction, doesn't it?

It's not. This is exactly what happens at the free clinic where I volunteer a few hours a week now. Our patients have no insurance. Most of them work full-time, and many of them work more than 40 hours a week. Still, they don't make enough money to afford health insurance, and they're not eligible for Medicaid or Medicare.

I serve as an internist at this clinic, the first line, primary care doctor for patients. We do prevention—vaccinations, cancer screenings, screening for infectious diseases, heart disease, diabetes. We treat common medical problems, and the volunteer specialists treat more complex ailments. There are dozens of us who volunteer our time—doctors in every specialty you can think of, nurses, dentists, physical therapists, psychologists, health educators, medical translators, and social workers. Even IT consultants to help with the ancient, clunky electronic medical records. Most of us are partially or fully retired from our day jobs in healthcare.

Donations of services come from hospital systems and other medical facilities, and equipment and medications are donated by drug companies or charitable organizations. The few paid employees of our clinic work hard to keep all these moving parts running smoothly.

As much as a free clinic meets the tremendous needs of a community, it is far from a perfect solution to medicine's ills. There are narrow criteria to qualify for our services; if there weren't, there wouldn't be enough to go around. Patients can't choose their doctors here—they are assigned to the first doctor with an available appointment in the needed discipline. Sometimes patients move from one primary doctor to another because of scheduling issues. There are some tests and equipment and medication we don't have access to; sometimes, we have to make do. Patients may have to wait weeks or months for a non-urgent service. Still, overall, it works. Most of our patients get the care they need.

The volunteers are, of course, self-selected. We share the conviction that the U.S. healthcare system is unfair, and that basic prevention and treatment should be a right, not a privilege that is out of reach for so many. My time seems like such a tiny contribution, especially when I think about how easy it has always been for me and my children to access care due to our expensive commercial insurance.

I know it shouldn't be this way. I know there are many in this country who don't want to pay more taxes, who don't want to 'subsidize' the healthcare of those who can't afford medical insurance, but it seems so obvious to me that healthier communities and a healthier population is good for all of us. I also know health is about much more than adult healthcare. Many of the patients we see at the free clinic, maybe most of them, develop diabetes, hypertension, and heart disease at a relatively young age. Compared to wealthier people, these patients are sicker, regardless of how hard they try to live healthy lives. So many factors contribute: the lack of access to care early in life, the lack of access to fresh fruits and vegetables, the stress of living with financial worries, discrimination, and uncertainty.

As a doctor, a session in free clinic feels like a breath of fresh air. My schedule leaves me plenty of time for each patient. I can review medical records and lab studies before I enter the room. I speak with patients, often with the help of a translator, examine them, and formulate a care plan.

After two years as a volunteer, I know some of my patients pretty well. I know what work they do, who they live with, what they worry about. They ask me questions, and I answer. I don't feel like I need to rush out of the room and move on to the next person.

The doctors share a big work room where we do our charting. This common space allows us to make use of each other's knowledge and expertise. Another internist asks me about her chronic migraine patient, knowing I am up on the newest medications. I grab the dermatologist in the hallway to ask her to look at photos of my patient's rash. She offers to pop in and look for herself then suggests a treatment option.

This give and take feels familiar, something from the distant past. Years ago, I'd see lots of my colleagues in the halls of the hospital, at staff meetings, and at conferences. That was before everything started moving so fast that all we could do was sit in front of our computers and click away on keyboards in isolation. It was before the time when our only discourse occurred through EMR messaging or by email.

Here, in this clinic, I am the internist I remember being once, the one who knew more about her patients than the problem list in the EMR, who was happy to see each patient, who felt trusted by her patient's families. The internist who thought through problems and shared opinions with colleagues, who was motivated to read about a new diagnosis or treatment. It reminds me that medicine's magic can still happen, even if there are some inherent miseries. It reminds me why I chose a medical life all those years ago.

There are, of course, some miseries here. Sometimes patients don't follow recommendations, or they drink too much or don't want to quit smoking, or they refuse a COVID vaccine. Sometimes someone is very sick, and we can't get them better. But these are miseries that are part of practicing medicine, the ones I expect. The EMR is frustrating. If I forget to click on "save," my work disappears and I have to start over. Some of the diagnoses I need are not in the database. Occasionally, I lose connection with the server, and I have to wait for help from the IT volunteer. I can live with these issues; it's nothing compared to fighting with insurance companies or being chastised about my billing.

Ironically, all of us are quite cost-conscious in free clinic. We don't need insurance administrators breathing down our necks to remember to use generic medications and to avoid unnecessary blood tests. We know we must conserve resources in order to serve as many patients as possible. We also know that over testing can hurt individual patients. Nevertheless, if a patient really needs a test, we order it, and it is carried out.

Here's the rub. This is my four-hour-a-week volunteer job, not real life. In real life (or IRL as they say on social media), nothing is free. IRL, nobody is going to hand medication to a patient who has no way to pay. IRL, a patient with medical insurance may not be able to get definitive treatment for a tooth infection because dental insurance is separate. Doctors and dentists all know dental care is inextricably linked to general health, but that doesn't change the bottom line. IRL, a patient with no insurance and no primary doctor may end up in an emergency room for the flu and later receive a bill that will leave them in debt for years to come. IRL, practicing internal medicine was dangerous to my mental and physical health, and I had to leave.

If only we could find a way to bring just a little part of this place into real life, it would be a start. It seems like it's not that big an ask. Let the doctors have a little more time with each patient. Give us some time and space to share knowledge and ideas. Let us decide what medications and tests a patient needs without authorization from insurance administrators who neither practice medicine nor know our patients. Pay nurses and social workers to do nursing and social work. Let us do our jobs.

Give us back some time and autonomy, and we'll keep more of our patients out of the E.R. and out of the hospital. In the long run, that will save money.

Give us a little more magic and a little less misery. It's not so much to ask.

FIFTEEN

Luck of the Draw

My husband's parents have grown old, ninety-one and eighty-nine this year. They live in an independent apartment within a senior living community in Florida. Though they have recently begun to lose their memories, their footing, and their nerve, they decline a move to assisted living. Mom falls; she is frail, has brittle bones and flaccid muscles, thin skin bruising the purple-blue of winter dusk under her perpetual Florida tan. Dad, a retired doctor, still demands deference. He wants to be in charge but has forgotten how to give orders.

The children—my husband and three siblings, scattered across the country—gather on video calls, bicker and wring their hands over care plans: home health aides, meals, doctor visits. Walkers, canes, PT, the weekly filling of pill boxes. The COVID pandemic has stretched space.

Once a short plane ride, the distance between my husband's parents and their children is sometimes as unfathomable as a trip to Bali, or maybe Mars, as the senior facility fluctuates in and out of COVID lockdown. The adult children are often forced to handle care arrangements over the phone.

I lurk, listening, in the corner of my husband's study. I could help, but no one asks my opinion, and I won't offer the solutions that aren't answers to the end of a life, the fact of flesh and bone. I won't tell them the care plan doesn't matter so much as they care enough to make one, that the right equipment can't reverse the years, can't change an inexorable trajectory.

Their anxiety bends time for me, folds it back twenty years, and I am a daughter again, coaxing her father to listen to reason. He will refuse help—the walker, the hearing aid—until he can no longer refuse. I know his compliance means we've lost. And then I am an orphan, throwing a shovel of dirt on his grave on a bright, clear April day that feels like a contextual error. My only sibling, the one who left me in charge, trails behind.

I want to say: *Be careful what you wish for. When they accept your ministrations, that is when you should worry. That is when to cry.* I don't. Let them believe that loose ends can be tied together, that tying a proper knot might keep the whole thing from unraveling.

The years fold back again, and I am a pregnant and motherless daughter, lifting her father from the kitchen floor after a fall. He will refuse the ambulance I have called. I'll clean his cuts myself, listen to his heart with my own stethoscope, believe I'm in control. I won't know this is only the beginning, that as my children's world grows, my father's will shrink to distant memories and a room with a hospital bed. It is better for me not to know this.

I want to say, *Let your father control what he still can. Give him space; that space will soon close on its own. Let it be.* But it might be better for them, as well, not to know this.

Time bends, doubles, and it is thirty years ago, half of my life ago. I am a new mother at her own mother's funeral, trembling but dry-eyed, delivering a eulogy. I have just finished medical training; I am good at compartmentalizing. Later, over many years, I will grieve in shatteringly, searingly painful bouts.

I want to say, *Take heart, your mother lived to see her grandchildren graduate from college and even stand at the altar. She held her first great-grandchild. Maybe you will too.*

I want to say, *You are here, doing this together.* Be grateful for each other. I won't. I will refrain from pointing out the obvious—lives well-lived, some dreams realized, others relinquished to reality, the luck of the draw, that they pulled the long straw. The constant tick of the clock, the forward momentum, our own mortality made real by our parents' deaths. I have been mortal for such a long time now; I know they are missing nothing. No reason to rush them.

SIXTEEN

Reprise of Shedding My Coat
Part III
Untethered

In the summer of 2021, a little more than a year into the coronavirus pandemic, I longed to adopt a second dog. The dog we had, Eli, was a quiet little chihuahua mix. He made a wonderful lap dog, but with his short legs and anxious, timid nature, he was not an ideal walking companion; if we tried to take him farther than two blocks from the house, he'd sit down on the sidewalk and refuse to move. I needed a partner for trail walks and long strolls, and it seemed like Eli could use some dog company.

I began searching Petfinder.com for a suitable dog—medium-sized, good with other dogs, no serious health problems. Everyone was snatching up rescues at that point, and I was coming up empty until I saw a picture of Sanderson. One-year-old, twenty pounds or so, and with a soft ginger-and-white coat, he looked like a small version of a Collie, the dog of my childhood dreams (I grew up without dogs because my father was allergic, but I desperately wanted one from the time I was five). Sanderson's foster mother said he'd likely spent months running loose on the streets of Houston, Texas, eating garbage and drinking rainwater to survive before the rescue picked him up. Unable to place him in Texas, where people were less open to adopting strays, they arranged a foster family in Connecticut while he awaited a permanent home.

"He's doing great now," she told me. "He's resilient and resourceful. He's really a happy guy." I knew then Sanderson was going to be my walking partner.

When Larry and I brought him home to Philly from Connecticut, the first thing he did was run away. I was leaning into the back seat of the car, trying to put a leash on him, when he squeezed past me and bolted into the neighborhood. Who could blame him? We'd removed him from the only home he'd known and put him in the car with strangers for two hours. It took the help of several neighborhood children on bicycles to locate and recapture him. But after a night with Eli, a few treats, and some intensive petting, he decided he was going to stay with us after all.

A few months later, I was out walking Sanderson, now nicknamed Sandy, in our neighborhood when the hook on his leash, the one that attaches the leash to collar, malfunctioned and detached. At first, finding himself free to run, Sandy bounded down the sidewalk and across the street (thankfully a quiet street at a time when there was no traffic). Then he stopped suddenly and looked around. He reversed direction and sprinted towards me and then away again. He repeated this pattern three or four times before he finally stopped running and walked halfway to me. There, he stood, in the middle of the street, waiting for me to come to him. He sat down and remained still as I reattached his leash.

Months out from my exit from my academic internal medicine practice, I felt the way I imagine Sandy must have felt the day he got loose: untethered, unsure, a little unhinged. No longer leashed to my responsibilities—the 24/7 needs of a too-large, too-sick patient population, the relentless flow of inbox messages, and the thousands of administrator-generated tasks—I was free to run, light, a weight lifted from me, until I realized what else I'd come unhooked from. Medicine had been my identity and my community, the hub of my daily existence for over three decades. Without it, I felt like I had no goals, no purpose, no center. I wasn't sure who I was or what I would do.

I approached and avoided medicine repeatedly for half a year, looking at part-time jobs and emailing back and forth with recruiters, but always retreated well before any potential position might become reality. Entirely disconnected from clinical practice, I longed for my stethoscope, but I was afraid to commit to picking it back up. I feared going back to the prison of overwork, stress, and helplessness I'd managed to escape.

The unexpected offer of a part-time job in urgent care, a job I hadn't even applied for, finally became the compromise I could live with. No inbox, no night on-call (both good), and no long-term patient relationships (a little sad). It was like a long, loose leash connecting me to clinical care. A tether I could sever at any point without much consequence.

My ambivalence and unwillingness to return to a life tightly tied to medicine and to my patients was accompanied by a deep sense of shame. It was no surprise to feel that way. I'd hitched myself to my professional identity a very long time ago, during years of medical education and residency training that were heavily laced with shaming techniques.

Once doctors are past training, shaming doesn't stop. Healthcare institutions often use shame to rein in doctors and extract the maximum amount of work possible from them. Take the use of practice metrics to create report cards comparing one doctor to another. Everyone can see who is meeting the desired thresholds for productivity, monetization, and data entry as well as who isn't.

I can recall many times I felt shamed during my time as a physician employed by one health system or another. For example, if we were short a medical assistant, we also might be asked to room our own patients, take their vital signs, and enter the triage data into the electronic medical record, a process that took up time I didn't have. When I objected to performing someone else's job in addition to my own, I got answers like, "Dr. G. rooms her own patients and doesn't complain." Or even, "What's the problem? Do you think you're too good to room a few patients?" Then I would wonder about myself. Why am I so demanding? Do I think I'm too good? Why can't I just be a team player? I was shamed not just into doing the work, but also into questioning my own motivation.

More and more, I got the message that I, rather than institutional and office dysfunction, was the problem. When I heard from several patients that they'd left phone messages for the office and never received responses, I shared my concern with an office manager, who told me all the messages left had been handled, so I must be mistaken, or perhaps my patients weren't being truthful. At a meeting about scheduling, I pointed out that I was often moving from my morning patient session to my afternoon session without having any time to eat or use the restroom. I asked that we talk about how to build in a short break. An administrator looked at me with a frown and said, "You seem awfully concerned with eating lunch," as though I were the only doctor who'd ever needed to eat. I felt ashamed again, shamed out of asking for something that is a basic human need, as well as shamed into questioning myself and my work ethic.

I also felt ashamed of my loneliness when I was at work, surrounded by other people. Colleagues didn't seem to feel isolated the way I did; everyone was busy and focused on their work. They seemed fine without conversation, without other doctors to run their thoughts by. Why was I so needy? Much later, maybe a year after I left, a specialist whose office had been just upstairs from mine told me she'd had the same experience. Her colleagues had rarely spoken to her, and it had worn on her enough that she, too, had left. It wasn't only me, but I didn't know that then.

Now, no longer an employed doctor with my own group of patients, I continued to feel ashamed, though for different reasons. The *Merriam-Webster Dictionary* defines shame as, "A painful emotion caused by consciousness of guilt, shortcoming, or impropriety." There. All the above. Guilt because I left my patients and abandoned a struggling specialty of primary care, even though, at one time, I had gotten great satisfaction from it. Shortcoming, because I wasn't tough enough and selfless enough to suffer stoically, silently, valiantly. Impropriety because breaking ranks felt taboo, like going AWOL from the military, and because I wasn't playing the game anymore. I'd stopped keeping my head down and trying to please everyone around me in those last months of practice. I hadn't been able to please anyone. At times, I hadn't been remotely pleasant.

Shame is a complicated, raw emotion doctors don't generally talk about. We like to keep up the façade of calm and cool, of knowing it all, of having it all under control. We might be roiling cauldrons of stress and worry and fatigue inside, but we're not showing it. Not to our patients, and, for the most part, not to each other. Shame is way too messy an emotion for the physician community.

The ambivalence and shame I continued to feel was exhausting and uncomfortable. I felt alone in it, like the only person who'd ever thrown in the towel but wasn't sure they wouldn't need it back. I kept wondering what all the other doctors who managed to stay in their jobs knew that I didn't.

It wasn't long, though, before I began getting phone calls and emails that changed my thinking. In fact, it seemed there were a lot of other physicians out there who thought that *I* knew something *they* didn't.

One call that sticks with me was from a colleague asking me to talk to her friend, D., a female subspecialist at a suburban Philadelphia health system.

"I'm afraid she's going to make herself sick with overwork," said my colleague. "Her practice partner left abruptly, and now the health system expects her to take care of her own patients, his patients, and all the hospital consults that were previously divided between them. It's been months, and they haven't come even close to replacing him."

"How can I help her?" I asked, truly believing I had no insights or knowledge that could inform her experience.

"She wants to leave this job. She could get another job in a flash, but she doesn't see that she has options. She's told them she can't keep up this pace, that they need to hire at least a locum tenens doctor (a doctor who accepts temporary assignments) to fill in, but they don't seem to be listening. You're an example of someone who left and found other options."

Still unsure that my story would be helpful, but worried about D. after hearing her situation, I called her. I caught her at 9 p.m. still in her office, completing charts.

"This is the third night this week I haven't been home to say goodnight to my kids," she told me. "My husband is handling it, but this has been going on for months, and I don't see an end. I'm sleeping at most five hours per night. Last week I started having chest pain. It's not my heart; it's just stress, or at least I think so."

"What have you told your administrators?" I asked her.

"I told them they need to hire someone."

"Did you give them a timeline? An ultimatum that you will resign if they don't get you help by a certain date?"

"I'm afraid to do that. It will make them angry. They think I should be able to handle all the patient care."

"What will they do if they get angry?" I asked.

"They might fire me."

"I don't think they can afford to fire you. You're doing double the work you signed on for, and there's nobody else to do it."

"Good point," D. admitted.

"What happens if you don't do some of the work?" I asked her.

"I can't do that. It would hurt the patients. I don't have that in me. That's why I'm trapped. They know I'm going to just do it."

"Have they offered to pay you more or give you something in return for this?"

"No! They haven't even said, 'Thank you.' In fact, they were nagging me about incomplete charts last week, so I went in to do them on Sunday. I know how much I'm doing, but somehow after I talk to administration, I always feel like I've done something wrong." Her voice rose in frustration.

"If they got help for you, would you want to stay at this job?" I asked.

"Actually, no. I wanted to look for a research job even before this happened. I thought I'd find one and then give notice a few months before my contract is up in a year. But now, I have no time or energy for a job search."

"Could you financially afford to be unemployed for a few months if you quit this job and then looked for a new one?" I prompted.

"I mean, well—I never thought about doing that. It seems risky. But yeah, we could easily live on my husband's salary and our savings for a little while."

"Okay. This is what you've told me. You can't take this much longer, it's making you sick, and giving you chest pain. Your employer isn't fixing the situation, or even attempting to make it more palatable. You don't want this job long-term, and you could survive for a short time without a salary. Is that all accurate?"

"Well, yes. When you say it like that, it sounds like I'm a fool for not quitting."

"I would never call you a fool. It's hard. We've been raised and trained and molded to be such good girls, to do what's right and not rock the boat. But your boat is sinking! I think you needed to hear back your own words!"

"What about my contract? They could penalize me for leaving before it's up."

"I guess they might try. But I think it's pretty clear that your contract was already violated when your work and your call doubled, and you got nothing for it except half a heart attack. I can recommend a good contract lawyer if you need one."

"I don't know. I just don't know. I'm going to think about it. I'll take the lawyer's information, though, if you don't mind."

I shared the contact via text.

"Well, you have my phone number. If you want to talk again, call or text me anytime," I said, ending our phone call.

When my dog Sanderson got loose from his leash, he was impulsive for a minute or so, but then decided on his own to return to me and to the leash. He willingly allowed me to reattach it. Sure, it might have been fun to run free for a bit, but in the end, he wanted and needed what he received when he remained tethered. His loyalty to me was not unconditional, though. In return he got shelter, food, treats, petting, and praise. He occasionally needed some correction, but I did it gently—no yelling or hitting, no shock collars. I didn't rub his nose in his own poop if he had a housebreaking accident. There was no shaming.

Sandy's treatment was consistent. He knew what to expect. Nobody changed the rules on him suddenly. His decision, it seems to me, made sense: the pros of being on leash outweighed the cons.

If I had treated Sandy less kindly, would he have come back to his leash? If he desperately needed what was on the other end (food and shelter), perhaps he would have returned to his captivity, even if he'd been hurt and shamed and saddened. But Sandy had been able to fend for himself before people took him in. He was resilient and resourceful. I suspect he would have fled if he'd found himself with a cruel human.

Of course, Sandy's a dog, and people are different—or maybe not so different, really.

A person desperately needing what's on the other end of the tether that is their job or their profession—the salary, the identity, a purpose—might choose that leash, even if shamed, hurt, and sad. But someone who can find the resources to run free? Why would they choose to be a captive?

The story I'd heard from D. was an eye-opener. I guess it's much easier to see clearly when you're looking at someone else's picture. As I viewed D.'s struggle to break free from her toxic work world, my own departure took on different meaning for me. It was healthy. It was self-preservation. It was an act of individual resistance against a broken system that was blithely burning through its most precious resource—its workers. I had no reason to be ashamed.

My cognitive process moved forward, but the insight didn't transfer to my emotional life at that point. When I thought about those final months in primary care, a time when I was not the best version of myself, I still felt the shame. I guess I wasn't fully healed after all.

In the ensuing weeks, D. didn't call me. I thought maybe I'd overstepped, pushed her too hard. Or that her employer had finally found her a new practice partner, and she was feeling better. I only hoped I hadn't made things worse for her.

It was a few months later that D. texted me and asked if I would meet her for coffee. Sitting at a local Starbucks sipping a skim latte, she told me she'd resigned with the help of the contract lawyer and was now on a three-week break before starting her new job in research at a pharmaceutical company.

"Let's talk about writing," she said. "I might have time for a hobby now."

Over the next couple of years, I had more conversations like the one with D.

A young colleague was swamped with administrative tasks. Other doctors in her practice had been granted extra administrative time and help from an assistant, but she'd been left to fend for herself. She knew it was unfair and that she had to speak up to her section chief, but when she'd tried, he'd accused her of complaining.

"Am I a complainer?" she asked me. "Part of me knows I'm not, but when he said that, I felt so ashamed of myself!"

A mid-career physician had developed a study protocol and applied for a grant on her own personal time. The grant brought money to her health system, and her section chief had promised her dedicated paid time to work on the study. But administrators vetoed that plan, saying the system couldn't afford for her to see less patients.

"Your grant isn't large enough for that," they told her, "and your patient volumes don't justify a raise."

"Other than making a profit for the institution, I feel like I'm worthless," she told me.

I could relate to every one of the stories I heard. I felt the stress, frustration, shame, and anger my colleagues carried. The conflicts seemed, on face value, preventable or at least remediable. But the administrators or doctors in leadership continually failed to address the concerns. I wanted to believe they were too busy or didn't understand how important even small issues could be for individual doctors. In truth, though, it seemed to me that they were more invested in the bottom line of their organizations than they were in physician satisfaction. That in turn appeared shortsighted, as doctor satisfaction often translates to patient satisfaction. To put it simply, happier and healthier doctors make for happier, healthier patients. Burned-out, exhausted, and dispirited doctors can't serve their patients well, and doctors who leave practice can't help them at all.

As surprised as I was to find myself in the role of confidante for other doctors, it was obvious to me that there was an unfilled need. Though I rarely had advice to offer, it was clear that talking to someone who understood the dynamics of medical practice and healthcare institutions provided relief to these doctors. It was more than just understanding the context. It was also that I provided a safe space for them. I had no personal stake in their stories, and I had no connection to their employment. They had nothing to lose with me.

I was happy to be the listening ear, but I also felt a little insecure about it. Those confiding in me might not know the whole of my saga. Didn't they realize that I had no answers? Weren't they aware of how badly it had all ended for me? That I was still carrying all that shame? What if I steered someone the wrong way or gave someone bad advice? Not everyone needed to leave medicine or their practice or their institution. The issues I heard about all had a variety of solutions, and in some cases, people just wanted to vent and had no need to act in any way.

I started to research the field of physician coaching, an adaptation of executive coaching in which specially trained physicians help other physicians to optimize their professional lives. Though physician coaching is a relatively new discipline, as physician stress and burnout have become more and more common in recent years, more physicians have been seeking coaches. I thought I might be able to help colleagues more if I had some training as a coach.

My research revealed that a coach is there to listen, support, and reflect, but not to give advice. Coaching clarifies values and goals and helps the client meet them. A good coach knows their client has the answers inside; their job is to assist the client in locating them. It immediately reminded me of my conversation with D., the physician doing double-duty. I hadn't needed to offer any opinion; I'd only reflected back to her what she'd told me. These were skills I'd like to learn and hone. Empowering other physicians to make good choices while protecting their values and priorities seemed to have no downside. Perhaps I could save others from the emotional suffering I'd gone through.

Coaching would not be an entirely altruistic pursuit for me, though. I thought if I could turn the mistakes and misdirection of my career into something positive, it could be another step in my own healing. Besides, coaching is a flexible professional pursuit—a way I might use my experience and knowledge on my own terms as I age. A way I might be a working part of the medical community beyond my clinical years.

I began looking into training programs, and in the fall of 2022, started a six-month online physician coach certification course, the most rigorous one I could find. Logging on to our first meeting, I knew I'd made the right decision. My cohort came from all over North America and had many different medical specialties and roles. But I somehow felt that I'd come home. These were my people. We meshed in a way I rarely had with colleagues, and the material we learned felt like a natural extension of everything in my career that had come before.

As part of training, my cohort spent countless hours paired up, practicing coaching techniques on each other. We were told to bring real-life issues to these practice sessions. During the time my practice partner acted as coach, I talked about that awful time before I walked away from primary care, and more specifically, my sense of shame and failure. My partner provided the safe space I needed to explore my feelings. She never said, "You shouldn't feel ashamed," but she clearly understood my feelings and their roots and also supported the decisions I'd made. The shame lifted a bit more with each coaching session. By the end of our program, I felt a little closer to being fully healed.

I also felt confident as a coach when the six-month training was complete. I was ready to combine this new skill set with my years of experience and hopeful that I'd help some other doctors find a little joy and satisfaction in their work instead of continuing to run on the hamster wheel that has become the centerpiece of modern medical practice.

With my newly acquired knowledge, I regretted that I hadn't found a coach for myself when I was really struggling at work. Given the circumstances, I don't think I would have made a different decision, but I might have made my choice with considerably less pain and stress.

I don't believe coaching is a panacea for the ills of the U.S.

healthcare system. I think it can serve as just one form of support for doctors and other healthcare workers trying to navigate the current insurance-based system. It's hard to work in a system that looks at health and illness as a money-making enterprise for insurers, medical institutions, and the administrators who work for those entities, and thus keeps doctors in a state of overwork.

The hamster-wheel is not what I signed up for when I chose medicine, and I don't think it's what my colleagues signed up for. It's not the way patients want their care meted out. Ultimately, doctors shouldn't accept this as the way we wield our education and experience. For now, though, it seems we have little recourse.

Sanderson and I are working with a trainer. I'm hoping he can learn not to bark and strain at the leash when larger dogs walk by, and that he can learn not to jump wildly up and down when he is excited.

"He's a really good dog," Alison, the trainer, tells me. "He walks nicely on the leash and listens to commands when he's calm. It's just when he gets anxious that these behaviors are cropping up. You need to pay attention to his anxiety level. Notice when he starts to stiffen up or breathe more heavily. That means he's stressed. If you can calm him before it escalates, things will go better. Try to figure out what he's reacting to. If you see a big dog coming towards you, get his attention and change course. If there's a frightening noise, don't lead him towards it. He'll learn to trust that you will protect him from harm. And of course, remember to praise him when he's doing a good job."

I've come to understand it's Sandy's job to walk calmly and

comfortably on a slightly loose leash, and it is my job to help him do that. He's tethered, and I'm at the other end of that tether, giving him encouragement and pointing him in the right direction. My job is to help him be successful. If we both do our jobs well, then we both win.

If only health systems could take a little piece of the theory that Alison taught me and apply it to their relationships with doctors. No, I am not saying doctors are like dogs or that patient care is not unlike walking on a leash. What I'm saying is certain aspects of animal physiology and animal behavior apply to humans in general, and human doctors more specifically. We are also creatures who have nervous systems and feelings. We function optimally when we're calm and confident, and when we are part of a system of mutual trust and caring.

It would be incredibly helpful if the hospital systems we work for paid attention to our collective stress levels and changed course when those levels began to escalate. We can't avoid stress completely in medicine; we are in the business of handling emergencies and urgent patient situations. But the stress could be kept to a dull roar if doctors got more administrative and clinical support when they need it.

It would also be a huge relief to doctors if we could state what we need to function well without being told that we are "complainers." It would go a long way if health administrators considered solutions to burnout, such as allowing doctors more control over their patient schedules rather than offering us mindfulness classes or yoga at lunchtime. For one thing, "lunchtime" doesn't happen for most physicians, and for another, it is just more for the physician to do—an insinuation that the source of burnout and stress is within the physician, that the physician needs to "fix" herself. Instead, it would help if systemic issues were acknowledged and addressed.

What if physicians and other healthcare workers were rewarded for jobs well-done more frequently, rather than receiving negative feedback about their metrics every week? That, too, might lessen the sense of isolation and beleaguerment that adds to the risk of burnout.

It would be a much larger move forward if the U.S. healthcare system as a whole stopped viewing the health and lives of human beings as a source of revenue and started seeing medical care for what it is: a combination of science and art, technology and human contact, an expensive but necessary undertaking that should be a right for everyone that we all are responsible to pay for, as a community, through taxes. Of course, here I am on a political soapbox. But I know there is no easy fix to the political divides that prevent us from doing what every other industrialized country has already done, and what has proven to improve the overall health of those nations.

I have a tattoo around my right ankle that reads, "Without hope the heart would break," a paraphrase of a quote by the Seventeenth Century philosopher, Thomas Fuller. Sometimes the practice of medicine in this country does break my heart. Still, I'm not without hope. While we battle negative, backward motion in reproductive health, racial disparities in medical care, and worsening physician shortages, positive changes are also afoot.

The recent expansion of the Affordable Care Act in forty-one U.S. states has extended access to care to hundreds of thousands of citizens who previously had no health coverage. This year the No Surprises Act banned unexpected bills for emergency care and scheduled care that falls out of network, but patients didn't choose, formerly a shockingly common practice. Much more needs to be done to protect patients from mercenary actions by insurers and hospital systems; if patients fall under heavy financial stresses in order to receive care, it significantly impedes the doctor-patient relationship and trust in the medical profession. It will drive some patients away from care entirely.

More good news: there are a few healthcare systems, mostly academic, scattered throughout the country that seem to understand the escalating stress physicians are experiencing. These institutions are creating robust physician wellness programs providing counseling, coaching, and sometimes services to help with errands and other tasks doctors struggle to get done in their day. It doesn't replace a decrease in workplace stressors, but it's a beginning.

On the provider side, younger doctors are beginning to rise up against exploitation as cheap labor by for-profit hospitals. Resident doctors around the country are beginning to unionize, especially after the worst days of COVID-19. During that time, they became frontline workers for eighty to one hundred hours a week, without adequate staff or protective equipment, and received no extra compensation. Some attending physicians are also unionizing, citing poor working conditions and lack of decision-making power as employees of hospitals.

While it may seem self-serving for doctors to protest their working conditions, improvements would also protect patients from understaffing, physician shortages, and suboptimal care from overextended and overwhelmed doctors.

I have hope that the younger attending doctors in practice, the residents who will soon be attendings, the med students who will soon be residents, and the pre-meds who will soon be med students all push hard against the system. Not just for better immediate working conditions, but also for the opportunity to be part of decision-making processes in hospital systems, and for the chance to lead the way to healthcare that is more focused on the health and well-being of all humans, including themselves. I have hope that they will see they, too, deserve to be happy and healthy. I have hope they will resist the culture of exploitation, subjugation, and shaming that has led to a generation of doctors who no longer feel full-hearted love for the practice of medicine.

Growth is hard. The situation may get worse before it gets better. Significant change won't happen in time for my generation of doctors to have a better life in clinical medicine. I'm not going back to work as a full-time doctor. But I'll be comforting, coaching, and cheering on my younger colleagues as they continue to work towards decreasing misery and rediscovering magic in medical practice.

Acknowledgements

Many, many people deserve thanks for making the writing and publication of this book a reality, and I can't possibly thank them all individually. Here are a few specifics that stand out:

First and foremost, thank you to my husband, Larry Kaplan, my partner in parenting wonderful children, parenting wonderful dogs, doctoring, educating, learning, celebrating, grieving, loving, and living. Larry has supported, encouraged, and cheered me on in my pursuit of writing. He has given me the time and space I need to write, has been the first reader of every page, and generously allows me to include his stories in my own.

Thank you to my adult children, Max and Maddy, for allowing me to write about them in these essays. They appear as infants and children in some of the stories though they have since grown to be wise and compassionate adults.

The Greater Philadelphia Writer's Wordshop has been a long-standing staple in my writing life. Many thanks to Alison Hicks Greifenstein and the members of this workshop for reading iterations of my essays, for their talent, and for their supportive, honest, and helpful suggestions.

I also owe thanks to the nonfiction mentors at Lesley University's MFA program, where some of this work was conceived. Pam Petro, Rachel Manley, Jane Brox, and Kyoko Mori were all instrumental in teaching me the art of the memoir-essay.

A heartfelt thanks to Minerva Rising Press for the opportunity to share these essays with a wider audience. A special thank you to Rebecca Beardsall, Minerva Rising's nonfiction editor, for her keen eye and wise counsel.

Last but not least, thank you to all the many patients who have entrusted me with their medical care and allowed me to be part of their lives. That trust, and the doctor-patient relationship, is precious. I fear for what medicine would become without it.

Acknowledgements of Previous Publications

"Bag of Bones and Box of Knees" –A previous version of this essay was published in Philadelphia Stories' Anthology *Prompted*, PS Books, 2010

"Oxy" – Published in *The Smart Set*, July 2021

"Dancing With Death" – Published in *Signal Mountain Review*, Fall 2022

"Dream Logic" – Published in *Minerva Rising*, Winter 2022

"Some Matters of Choice" – Published in the *Front Page of Open Arts Forum*, February 2022

"To A Patient" – Published in the *Annals of Internal Medicine* "on Being a Doctor" section, June 2018

"Tornado, Initial Encounter" – Published in *Pulse Magazine*, November 2020

"Detach" – Published in *HerStry*, August 2021

"Grow Old Along with Me" – Published in *Sweet Tree Review*, Winter 2022

"Luck of the Draw" – Published in *Stonecoast Review*, Winter 2022

---ABOUT THE AUTHOR---

Rosalind Kaplan

Rosalind Kaplan is a general internist and writer in Philadelphia. She earned her M.D. Degree from the University of Pennsylvania's Perelman School of Medicine in 1987, and her MFA in creative writing from Lesley University in 2020. Her first full-length memoir, *The Patient in the White Coat* (New York, NY, Kaplan Publishing) was published in 2010. Her essays can be found in a number of literary journals, including *Across the Margin, El Portal, Green Hills Literary Lantern, Minerva Rising, The Smart Set, Sweet Tree, Vagabond City* and others. She teaches medical humanities and writing at Thomas Jefferson/Sidney Kimmel Medical College. She has two adult children. When she is not working or traveling, she can be found at home or hiking with one of her two rescue dogs.

www.ingramcontent.com/pod-product-compliance
Lightning Source LLC
Chambersburg PA
CBHW030137170426
43199CB00008B/98